TUNE UP TO LITERACY

TUNE UP TO LITERACY

ORIGINAL SONGS AND ACTIVITIES FOR KIDS

DR. AL BALKIN

AMERICAN LIBRARY ASSOCIATION
CHICAGO   2009

Dr. Al Balkin, Western Michigan University professor emeritus and composer/lyricist, has taught music at every level, from nursery school to graduate school. A consistent ASCAP award recipient, Dr. Balkin has written songs that have appeared on CBS television's *Captain Kangaroo* and on NBC, PBS, and CBS network radio. His song cycles, "We Live in the City" and "City Scene," broke new ground in elementary and middle school music, and his full-length theater piece, *The Musicians of Bremen*, has been performed over two hundred times. He wrote the music for America's first production of *The Hobbit* as well as several off-Broadway children's musicals. A graduate of Indiana University and Teachers College, Columbia University, where he received his EdD, Dr. Balkin has dedicated his career to arts-generated, multidisciplinary learning, exemplified by his songs, workshops, and articles, which have appeared in *Principal* and *Music Educators Journal*. He also coauthored the textbook *Involvement with Music* (1975).

The paper used in this publication meets the minimum requirements of American National Standard for Information Sciences—Permanence of Paper for Printed Library Materials, ANSI Z39.48-1992. ∞

Library of Congress Cataloging-in-Publication Data
Balkin, Alfred.
 Tune up to literacy : original songs and activities for kids / Al Balkin.
  p. cm.
 ISBN 978-0-8389-0998-0 (alk. paper)
 1. Children's libraries—Activity programs. 2. Children's songs, English—United States. 3. Language arts (Preschool) 4. Language arts (Primary) 5. Music in education. I. Title.
Z718.3.B35 2009
027.62'5–dc22
                                                                      2009008151

ISBN-13: 978-0-8389-0998-0

Printed in the United States of America
13 12 11 10 09   5 4 3 2 1

CONTENTS

 Recordings of the songs are available on the book's website, along with the sheet music: www.ala.org/editions/extras/balkin09980.

FOREWORD

I never considered myself a professional musician, but I have always used music in my children's story programs. I was a children's librarian for nearly twenty years, and today I still hit the road as a musically inclined storyteller. I don't have any statistics on the advantages of including music and literature-related activities, but I have hundreds of anecdotal experiences of children's eyes lighting up when they join me in song immediately after hearing a favorite story. I started with simple nursery rhymes but over the years grew comfortable singing more complex songs that featured the different aspects of a child's life: songs about family, friends, animals, concepts, and holidays. Because there were so few resources that taught me how to combine music with literary development, I had to find my own musical ideas. That's when I began writing my music books. I'm so glad that *Tune Up to Literacy* by Al Balkin is now on the market. It helps not only those nonmusicians who are interested in learning to add music to their story programs but also folks with extensive musical backgrounds.

Over the years I've conducted several workshops on ways to incorporate music into literacy programs. I've met several librarians and teachers who consider themselves nonmusicians. I've always challenged them to get out of their comfort zones and give music a chance. Many have done so. These are some of the folks who will find many new great ideas in this book. I've also talked to several librarians and teachers who have been musical all their lives. They sing, play guitar and piano, and read music. They are happy to include music in their children's programs and are constantly looking for new ideas and challenges. Al Balkin has not only included the scores for each song but also added dozens of musical and literacy tips.

I know that this book will find a home in public libraries as well as the classroom and school libraries. Public children's librarians will find fun activities in *Tune Up to Literacy* to share with their young charges. "March of the Alphabet," "At the Library," and "Stretch Your Imagination" are just a few of the stimulating songs that children's librarians can use to interact with children simply by playing the recordings from the website (www.ala.org/editions/extras/balkin09980). Teachers will no doubt have plenty of musical ammunition on hand as they teach kids about the various aspects of grammar. Take a look at "Call on a Verb," "A Syllable," "Nounsense," and more.

This book is not only for children's librarians and classroom teachers. Music teachers, child-care providers, and parents will also find it helpful. Librarians—be ready to recommend this resource to all adults who are looking for musical methods to make literature come alive for children.

Rob Reid
Author of *Children's Jukebox* and *Something Musical Happened at the Library*

PREFACE

As a boy growing up in the Boston area, my favorite activities were playing baseball, playing the piano (music, not scales!), and looking up new words in my pocket dictionary, which I carried with me everywhere but to baseball. I don't play baseball anymore. I do still play the piano. I still look up new words in the dictionary. I love music, I love words, and these two passions led to my writing songs, mostly for children, but not patronizingly childlike. Children respond to quality.

Nothing deserves more educational priority than a secure grounding in literacy. To read, write, and talk effectively is the key to communication for academic and life success. Add to this the ability to really listen. *Tune Up to Literacy* is a celebration in song of those skills and understandings crucial to communicating in our language. It presents the basic building blocks such as the alphabet, nouns, pronouns, verbs, adjectives, sentences, singular or plural, and so on. It also celebrates the virtues, the rewards, the pure joy of learning. Aided by the activities, the songs aim to reveal the essence of basic concepts as well as explore them in depth.

ACKNOWLEDGMENTS

The composer gratefully acknowledges the following contributions:

First and foremost, the dedicated and meticulous attention to detail of my wife, Rita (though a nonmusician), in transcribing these songs from manuscript to computer program. Without her efforts, tenacity, and remarkable skills, the *Tune Up to Literacy* project might be languishing in educational limbo rather than enlivening language learning in schools and libraries throughout our nation.

Dr. Mary A. Cain, an esteemed colleague and friend at Western Michigan University, a superb teacher and educational beacon, for her early contributions to the Teaching Guide, philosophical insights, and genuine concern for the program's success.

My colleagues, students, and friends throughout the country, and throughout the years, for their constant encouragement, support, and always enlightening dialogue.

And now, a new colleague and friend, Christopher L. Rhodes, acquisitions editor for ALA Editions, whose vision, sensitivity, and enterprising spirit recognized something unique in *Tune Up to Literacy* and who decided to publish this special edition. His thoughtful, steady guidance and genuine respect for the composer's ideas and feelings made for a most rewarding working relationship.

My thanks to ALA Editions managing editor, Christine Schwab; marketing manager, Jill Davis; eagle-eyed freelance copy editor, Carolyn Crabtree; editorial assistant, Eugenia Chun; designer, Casey Bayer; and those contributors unknown to me, but appreciated.

CONSIDERATIONS AND TIPS

Following is some brief advice for anyone who is using the songs and activities of *Tune Up to Literacy* to enhance, enlarge, and motivate the language arts education and lives of children. Included with the songs in *Tune Up to Literacy* is a wide-ranging collection of interdisciplinary, often creative activities, which include art, music, and movement. The suggested activities are precisely that—suggested. Librarians, teachers, parents, and others will find ideas that work best for them according to their own personality, background, training, objectives, and teaching styles.

CONSIDERATIONS

Each song unit either addresses a specific language arts concept (e.g., "Call on a Verb") or supports the language arts curriculum motivationally (e.g., "Learn to Read").

[WEB] Using the songs from the website (www.ala.org/editions/extras/balkin09980), librarians can effectively present the program regardless of musical ability. Collaboration with a music teacher can add a unique dimension and focus.

Each song is a total and clearly defined instructional unit that can stand alone.

This is not a supplemental program, but a true tool for reaching out and heightening children's mental abilities using a vehicle that children truly love. It *is* curriculum.

The songs and activities are conceptually cross-graded, and either or both can be plugged in wherever and whenever appropriate to the program content or curriculum.

[WEB] Parents can easily participate in *Tune Up to Literacy*. For instance, with the songs from the website, a car trip can become a learning experience. For parents as well, this is a teaching guide.

Though the song units all have literacy-based objectives, many of them have multidisciplinary implications, such as social studies, mathematics, science, art, and so on. These curricular connections can easily be developed and add breadth to the program.

Many of the songs have life messages that help children grow. They not only learn literacy concepts but also gain a better sense of being, doing, thinking, and creating and develop a greater awareness of all about them.

Many of the songs are interactive and call for varying levels of response ranging from essentially rote to considerable critical and creative thinking.

Many of the songs have strong connections to other songs in the program. All the songs have obvious connections to phonics.

The songs lend themselves readily to art, drama, and movement experiences.

TIPS

Librarians responsible for children's programming will find the songs musically satisfying, stylistically varied, and easily adaptable to entertaining and enlightening performance with many sing-along opportunities. The songs also lend themselves richly to music concept development.

Repeat the songs consistently after you introduce them. The concepts require constant reinforcement, and the children react positively to the familiarity of the tunes. A variety of visual aids helps to amplify the songs' impact.

If the children do not sing the whole melody, they can often sing the chorus or small segments of the melody that reinforce the idea.

Reading the lyrics to the children while playing the music will provide an enriching experience. The melodies are, of course, very important and desirable to perform, but the concepts and rhythm of the words are . even more important pedagogically. When introducing songs, let the children guess upcoming rhymes.

Before introducing a new song, play the instrumental version in the background while the children are engaged in other activities.

Play the songs from the website as background music so that children become familiar with the melodies without active attention. **WEB**

Use specific instrumentals for rhythmic and movement activities, storytelling, pantomime, and poetry reading.

SONGS

MARCH OF THE ALPHABET

Music & Lyrics by Al Balkin

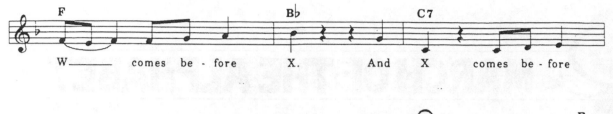

W_____ comes be - fore   X.   And   X   comes be - fore

Y.   And   Y   comes be - fore   Z.   Fi - nal - ly.

Alternate versions   *1.And   Z   comes af - ter   Y.   Now, good - bye.*
                           2.And   A   comes be - fore   B.   Fi - nal - ly.

LYRICS

1. A comes before B.
   And B comes before C.
   C comes before D.
   And D comes before E.
   Keep on marching.

2. E . . . F / F . . . G / G . . . H / H . . . I.
   Keep on marching.

3. I . . . J / J . . . K / K . . . L / L . . . M.
   Keep on marching.

4. M . . . N / N . . . O / O . . . P / P . . . Q.
   Keep on marching.

5. Q . . . R / R . . . S / S . . . T / T . . . U.
   Keep on marching.

6. U comes before V.
   And V comes before W.
   W comes before X.
   And X comes before Y.
   And Y comes before Z. Finally.

ALTERNATE VERSION 1

B comes after A.
And C comes after B.
D comes after C.
And E comes after D.
Keep on marching.
Follow same pattern.
And Z comes after Y.
Now, good bye.

ALTERNATE VERSION 2

Y comes before Z.
And X comes before Y.
W comes before X.
And V comes before W.
Keep on marching.
Follow same pattern.
And A comes before B. Finally.

ACTIVITIES

Children love to move. They especially like to march. This song allows them to march while they learn the letters of the alphabet in the proper order and with a considerable degree of independence. The letters are separated in the song and have logical connections.

1. As you play the recording, have the children keep the beat by alternating their left foot and right foot while sitting or standing.

2. Have children open and close their fists to keep the beat with the music. Do this with both hands or one hand at a time.

3. Follow the same basic procedure as in activity 2, but change the open and closed fist positions when the letter changes (open A, closed B; closed B, open C; open C, closed D; etc.).

4. Keep the beat with individual fingers of one hand (thumb is 1). Change the finger when the letter changes:

       1111, 2222; 2222, 3333; 3333, 4444; etc.
        A   B;   B   C;   C   D

   Repeat with the opposite hand and with both hands together.

5. Follow the same basic procedure as in activity 4, but do not keep the beat. Change the finger only when the letter changes. Except for A and Z, all letters will hold for eight counts.

6. Follow the same basic procedure as in activity 3, but vary the body movement and body part(s) throughout the song, changing completely with the introduction of each new letter. Invite children to create their own movement changes to accompany letter changes. This may be planned in advance or done spontaneously. In either event, the child who contributes a particular movement can be the leader for that movement.

7. Make letter banners or posters and give one letter to each child. Have the children march in place to the song. As the children march in place, have them raise their letters above their heads when their letter is sounded. Next, have them march around the room with each child stepping off holding his or her letter high as it is sung. The children are lined up in letter order and march in place until moving forward when their letter is sung.

8. Put each letter on a card. Place all the cards on the floor and have the children take turns finding any letters from the song that they recognize. When they find one, have them hold it up and announce it to the group. Continue until every child has a letter. Now have the children try to arrange themselves in alphabetical order as you play the song (vocal version).

9. Have children use their bodies as percussion sources by using their open hands to gently strike different parts of their bodies as the letter changes.

10. As the recording plays, have children stand and write each letter in the air as it is sounded. Try to do this activity as rhythmically and artistically as possible.

11. Using the instrumental version, sing the song this way: "B comes after A. And C comes after B. D comes after C." and so on. Combine this version of the song with some of the accompanying movements already described.

12. Sing "March of the Alphabet" backward using the instrumental version (e.g., "Y comes before Z. And X comes before Y.").

13. Create letter collages using letters cut from magazines, or cut out pictures that represent words beginning with certain letters (e.g., a picture of a ball for the letter B).

VOWEL MAMBO

Music & Lyrics by Al Balkin

Vowelfully

*Repeat ⊕ ad libitum with fadeout.
When finished with repetitions, go to Fine.

LYRICS

A E I O U. A E I O U. A E I O U.

A E I O U. A E I O U. A E I O U.

Doing the vowel mambo.

A E I O U.

Doing the vowel mambo.

That's the dance we do.

A E I O U.

Vowel mambo.

Sing the vowel sounds that we know.

Repeat from beginning.

A E I O U. A E I O U. A E I O U.

Repeat ad libitum until ending.

Ending: A E I O U. A E I O U. A E I O U.

ACTIVITIES

This pulsating song gets everybody up and moving and helps children become familiar with the basic vowels of English. The song enables beginning readers to learn the names of the vowels in a fun context and reinforces their understanding of letter symbol–sound relationships.

1. Introduce the mambo as one of many Latin American dances. Teach the children a few basic mambo steps. Play "Vowel Mambo" and guide the children through the steps they have learned. This works especially well in the coda section.

2. Make several vowel card sets on large pieces of poster board, using a different color for each vowel. Give each child a vowel card and ask groups of five to flash their cards each time they hear their vowel. Ask three different groups of children to flash their cards during one of the three recurring melodic phrases using the A-E-I-O-U pattern. A fourth group might perform the once-only A-E-I-O-U phrase at the end.

3. Make children aware that the three recurrent A-E-I-O-U melodic phrases follow an up-down-up pattern. Point out, using appropriate actions, that phrases 1 and 2 move in opposite directions, and that phrases 1 and 3 use exactly the same notes with a slight variation in timing. Let children discover that difference and discover that the ending A-E-I-O-U phrase uses repeated notes followed by a down-up movement. Compare the ending phrase to phrases 1, 2, and 3.

4. Sing the song with the equivalent vowel sounds in Spanish.

5. Point out that the vowel sounds of the letters A-E-I-O-U usually do not sound that way in words by themselves. They are helped by other letters that create the long vowel sound (e.g., "use" needs *e* at the end so it will not sound like "us"; "aim" needs *i* in addition to *a* so it will not sound like "am"). Sing the song with long-vowel words instead of vowels only (e.g., day, tree, pie, glow, use). Explore the Rhyme-a-ton at the end of this book for more combinations.

6. Have children hold their hands up in the air. Assign numbers to their fingers. Thumbs are 1 and the other fingers are 2 through 5.

Using small pieces of construction paper, make two sets of the A-E-I-O-U sequence. Let each child arrange the pieces so that the fingers of each hand can comfortably touch them in order. Tape the letters down. Have the children say or sing the vowel sequence slowly at first and, as they sound each vowel, touch the proper letter. First, work with the right hand alone, then the left hand, then alternate hands, and finally both hands together. Before doing this activity on the table or floor, have the children practice it in the air.

7. Make several sets of footprints with a vowel on each footprint. Place the footprints around the room. When you call out the vowel sound, have the children find that vowel on the floor and stand on the footprint. Vary the activity by having each child place other body parts (e.g., elbow, hand, knee) on the footprint.

8. Cut out large vowel letters from construction paper. Pin or tape one vowel to each child. Arrange children in groups of five with each member of the group wearing the same vowel letter. Play the song. Tell each group to move forward when its letter is sounded.

9. Make a set of bingo cards using uppercase and lowercase vowels. Cards should be three squares across and three down. Call out vowels and play until someone has three in a row. Each winner must call out the three sounds of her or his winning card correctly. The capital letters stand for the long sounds, and the lowercase letters represent the short sounds.

10. As children listen to *Vowel Mambo*, they can form each vowel with their bodies, holding each one for two measures (A=2 measures, E=2 measures, etc.).

AT THE LIBRARY

Music & Lyrics by Al Balkin

Librarily

You can meet King Tut AT THE LI - BRA - RY.
Can go back in time AT THE LI - BRA - RY.

Learn to build a hut at the li - bra - ry. You can
Does - n't cost a dime at the li - bra - ry. You can

climb Pike's Peak at the li - bra - ry. See an an - cient Greek at the li - bra - ry. Meet a
fly a plane at the li - bra - ry. See in - side the brain at the li - bra - ry. Watch a

ritard last time

des - ert sheik at the li - bra - ry. At the li_____ bra__
mon - soon rain at the li - bra - ry. At the li_____ bra__

1) C

ry.
ry.

2) C

ry.

Note: See additional verses on page 12.

LYRICS

1. You can meet King Tut at the library.
   Learn to build a hut at the library.
   You can climb Pike's Peak at the library.
   See an ancient Greek at the library.
   Meet a desert sheik at the library.
   At the li-bra-ry.

2. Can go back in time at the library.
   Doesn't cost a dime at the library.
   You can fly a plane at the library.
   See inside the brain at the library.
   Watch a monsoon rain at the library.
   At the li-bra-ry.

3. See a movie set at the library.
   Maybe win a bet at the library.
   You can hear Chopin at the library.

   Meet a Scottish clan at the library.
   Visit Peter Pan at the library.
   At the li-bra-ry.

4. You can sail the Nile at the library.
   View the latest style at the library.
   Wade the Rio Grande at the library.
   Walk the Holy Land at the library.
   Knowledge on demand at the library.
   At the li-bra-ry.

5. Check out books for home at the library.
   After touring Rome at the library.
   Stacks of books so tall at the library.
   Books from wall to wall at the library.
   It's a learning mall at the library.
   At the li-bra-ry.

ACTIVITIES

The true heart and soul of the learning experience is the library. It symbolizes the wonders of learning: "Stacks of books so tall at the library. Books from wall to wall at the library. It's a learning mall at the library." Today's libraries are also giant repositories of electronic information. Computers, videotapes, audiotapes, CDs, DVDs, and myriad other audiovisual devices invite and motivate students to expand their horizons by exploring the world at their fingertips. This song aims to heighten and brighten that desire.

1. Let the children know it is their library, and they can come whenever they need to or want to.

2. Let them know that the library is a center for fun as well as education. In the philosophy of one county library, "The library is for learning, for leisure, and for life."

3. Introduce the children to finding books on the computer and provide hands-on experiences.

4. Acquaint the children with the library's computer games.

5. Show the children examples of different categories of books (fiction, nonfiction, biographies, autobiographies, science, geography and travel, dictionaries, different types of reference works, etc.).

6. Have the children practice finding examples of the various categories mentioned in activity 5.

7. Make clear that borrowing books is a free service available to anyone who has a library card. Explain that there may be fines for late returns. Make sure the children know how long they may borrow different types of books (some may be kept longer than others). Stress responsibility.

8. Tell the children about your library's special programs, such as magic shows, puppet shows, music performances, storytimes, poetry readings, and so on. Reinforce the concept that the library is a place where they can learn to love learning and have fun doing it.

9. Have children discuss the meaning of the sentence, "It's a learning mall at the library."

BETTER THAN TV

Music & Lyrics by Al Balkin

Warmly and with movement

BET - TER THAN T V, I love a sto - ry that some - bo - dy reads to me. What's the tale to - night? Please won't you tell me be - fore we turn out the light. Sto - ry old or new, I love the time I spend read - ing a - long with you. BET - TER THAN T V, I love a sto - ry that's read to me.— BET-TER THAN T V, I love a sto - ry.— I love a sto - ry.—

I love a sto - ry ⎯⎯⎯ you read for me. ⎯⎯⎯

You read for me. ⎯⎯⎯

ritard on last time　　　*repeat ad libitum*

You read for me. ⎯⎯⎯　　You read for me.

LYRICS

Better than TV,

I love a story that somebody reads to me.

What's the tale tonight?

Please won't you tell me

Before we turn out the light.

Story old or new,

I love the time I spend reading along with you.

Better than TV,

I love a story that's read to me.

Repeat.

Better than TV,

I love a story.

I love a story.

I love a story you read for me. You read for me. You read for me. You read for me. *(Repeat ad libitum.)*

ACTIVITIES

Today's parents, overburdened by extra responsibilities and worried by economic problems, are inevitably tempted to sit children in front of the television. Child development authorities express great concern about the overuse of inappropriate television. Moreover, parents often do not know more amenable experiences to substitute for TV, are often unaware that literacy begins at home, and do not understand the importance of reading to children. This song uses feeling to address that problem. Outcomes include added children's and parents' awareness of sharing literacy with each other, along with an increased involvement in shared book reading, both inside and outside the home.

1. Help children select books that they can read at home. Suggest that parents sit down with their children and listen to how well they are learning to read.

2. Divide the group into pairs and give children time to read to each other. (Help each child choose the book he or she will read. It should be a book that the child has already practiced reading.)

3. In a group with a range of ages, arrange for older children to read books that they've practiced to younger children.

4. Make sure every child has a library card!

5. Let parents and children know about TV programs of educational value, which are designed to encourage reading.

6. Ask the children to watch a favorite TV program and count the number of books that they see during the program. Are any bookshelves shown on the program? Any magazines? Any library scenes? (These types of questions not only focus attention on details but also heighten children's powers of observation.)

SING A SIMPLE RHYME

Music & Lyrics by Al Balkin

*Create new verses by supplying additional rhyme
sounds with appropriate pairs of words (e.g. eam/team-
dream; orn/born-corn; ate/skate-great).

Copyright © 1992 by Al Balkin
Published by NOW VIEW MUSIC

LYRICS

Sing a simple rhyme like name and game.

Sing a simple rhyme. Each word ends the same.

Sing a simple rhyme like cat and hat.

Sing a simple rhyme. It's as simple as that.

The sound is o (oh). One word could be grow.

The sound is o. Another could be snow.

The sound is eed. One word could be read.

The sound is eed. Another could be need.

Sing a simple rhyme like name and game.

Sing a simple rhyme. Each word ends the same.

Sing a simple rhyme like cat and hat.

Sing a simple rhyme. It's as simple as that.

Now make up your own rhymes. Use the verse:
"The sound is _____. One word could be _____."

ACTIVITIES

"Sing a Simple Rhyme" will fundamentally improve the ways that children attend to sound patterns in words. Wordplay and word associations invite children to provide words that rhyme. The song offers explicit instruction on what a rhyme is (the words end with the same sound). It then gives directed practice in identifying a potential rhyming word ending and listening to words that rhyme with that ending. Outcomes of this song include a clear understanding of what a rhyme is, improved ability to hear and discover rhymes, and better word analysis skills.

1. Explore rhyming words and sounds. Say a word and see if the children can name a rhyming word. When they run out of spontaneous rhymes, put the rhyming sound(s) on a chalkboard or overhead projector and consult the Rhyme-a-ton for more words. After having fun finding rhyming words, experiment with rhyming sounds (e.g., ook, ug, ed). Let children invent words that rhyme and have them make up definitions for their new words.

2. Create silly, rhyming one-sentence stories (e.g., "The ape jumped over the tree to see what he could see."). Let the children identify the rhyming words. Invite them to create their own silly sentences and underline the rhyming words.

3. Cut out interesting pictures from magazines. Give each child a picture and provide an opportunity to make up a rhyming sentence about it.

4. Make a group poem by having the children rhyme every other line. Set up a simple rhyme scheme such as *aabb*. Then move to *abab* for contrast.

5. Play other songs or recite poems (even Mother Goose) and have the children raise two hands whenever they hear a rhyming word. Point out that the rhyming words usually occur at the ends of sentences.

6. Introduce limericks. These silly poems can be great fun for the group to make up

(e.g., "There once was a boy named Ted. / He had a brother named Ed. / They both liked to play / in the school yard each day. / They played with their new friend called Fred.") Help the children see that the rhyme scheme is *aabba*.

7. Play the Rhyme-mate game. Make a big deck of cards with two words per card. Shuffle the deck. Throw the cards on the floor and set up two-person teams to find as many rhymes as possible.

8. Have a scavenger hunt for rhyming objects or pictures or both, such as cat/hat; glass/brass; bear/pear; soap/rope; smile/tile; pan/fan. Write each item on a card and show the card when a team finds the object or picture.

9. Have children substitute new words with rhymes at the appropriate places in some familiar songs, such as "Three Blind Mice," "On Top of Old Smoky," "Yankee Doodle," "London Bridge," and so on. Words might relate to other topics being presented in your program or storytime.

10. Invite each child to stand beside another child whose first or last name rhymes with hers or his, such as Jill/Bill or Don/John. Most names won't rhyme, so encourage children to make up their own rhyming names or sounds.

11. Explain to the children that though words may rhyme, the letters of the rhyming words may be different, such as "read" and "need" found in the song. Let them know that English is a "funny" language in which spelling is not always consistent.

12. Use letters cut from magazines to make rhyming words and have the children post them about the room.

CALL ON A VERB

Music & Lyrics by Al Balkin

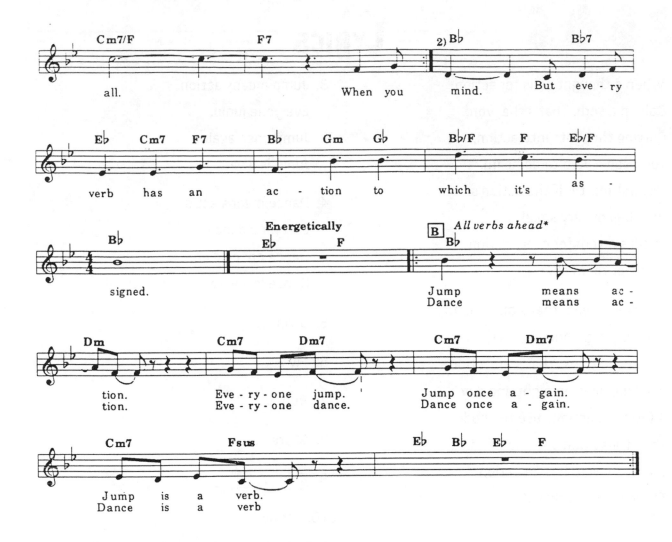

*Keep repeating **B** constantly changing verbs and actions
suggested by the children. (i.e. swim, fly, run, hop, etc.)

LYRICS

1. When a thought calls for action,
   Call on a verb. That's the word.
   Putting thoughts into action,
   You need a verb to be heard.
   Doesn't matter if the action's
   Very big, or very small.
   There's a verb for every action
   To cover them all.

2. When you read, that's an action.
   Not very big, some may say.
   When you think, that's an action.
   Thinking goes on night and day.
   A lot more actions use the body
   Than those that use the mind.
   But every verb has an action
   To which it's assigned.

3. Jump means action.
   Everyone jump.
   Jump once again.
   Jump is a verb.

4. Dance means action.
   Everyone dance.
   Dance once again.
   Dance is a verb.

5. Swim . . .

6. Fly . . .

7. Run . . .

8. Skate . . .

9. Ride . . .

10. Throw . . .

Repeat, using verbs and actions suggested by the children.

ACTITIES

Children love action. Most verbs connote obvious physical action, but there are quiet action verbs like reading, thinking, or just being. "Call on a Verb" makes clear the broad range of possibilities. It also presents a series of real action words that the children act out, and invites them to explore their creativity by adding their own verbs and accompanying actions. The outcome of the song is a secure understanding of what a verb is, and how it can indicate both "noisy" and "quiet" actions.

1. Play the song from the website (www.ala .org/editions/extras/balkin09980) and let the children act out the verbs in the song. Illustrate some.

2. Have children cut out pictures from magazines showing various actions. Let them identify the verbs and describe what is happening in each picture (e.g., "The woman is riding on her bicycle.").

3. Using each picture as the starting point, have children tell a story, emphasizing the verbs, about what took place before the picture and what is going to take place afterward.

4. Ask children to put several pictures together and create stories connecting the actions and people in the different pictures.

5. Create a story and then remove the verbs. Ask the children to fill in the blanks with verbs. Read the completed story back to them. See how many different versions the children can supply by using different verbs in the blanks (e.g., "The giant red dog _____ to the far side of the fence. He _____ over the fence and quickly _____ to his master.").

6. Make up two sets of flash cards. One set should be all verbs. The other set should be sentences with blanks where the verbs belong. Group children into pairs and hold up flash cards, one from each set. The first child to select an appropriate verb for the sentence being shown wins a point for his or her team. Acting out the verb wins another point.

7. Repeat activity 6, but incorporate sentences needing two verbs. Give two points for correct answers and two points for pantomiming the actions.

8. Show the children a simple verb (e.g., run, walk, look) and make a list of more interesting, more exciting, more precise substitutes (look = peer, view = squint). This is an excellent opportunity to introduce the concept of *synonym* and to explain how to find synonyms in a thesaurus. Though the children may be able to decipher the sounds of some of these synonyms, you should explain the shades of meaning various synonyms connote. This exercise not only gets children thinking of variety in language with extended possibilities in sound, look, and meaning but also gives them a new and valuable reference tool—the thesaurus.

9. Read a story aloud replacing the verbs with the word "buzz" or any other nonsense word or any sound you choose. Ask the children to supply a verb that makes sense (e.g., "The boy buzz [walks] along the street. He buzz [stops] at the store for an ice cream cone. He is buzz [eating] the ice cream when he buzz [sees] his sister. He buzz [shares] the rest of his cone with her.").

10. Divide the group into teams. Have each team create a new adventure hero and ask the children to describe and act out all the things the hero is able to do, such as leap tall buildings, run faster than a jet plane, or move mountains with one finger.

GET THE POINT

Music & Lyrics by Al Balkin

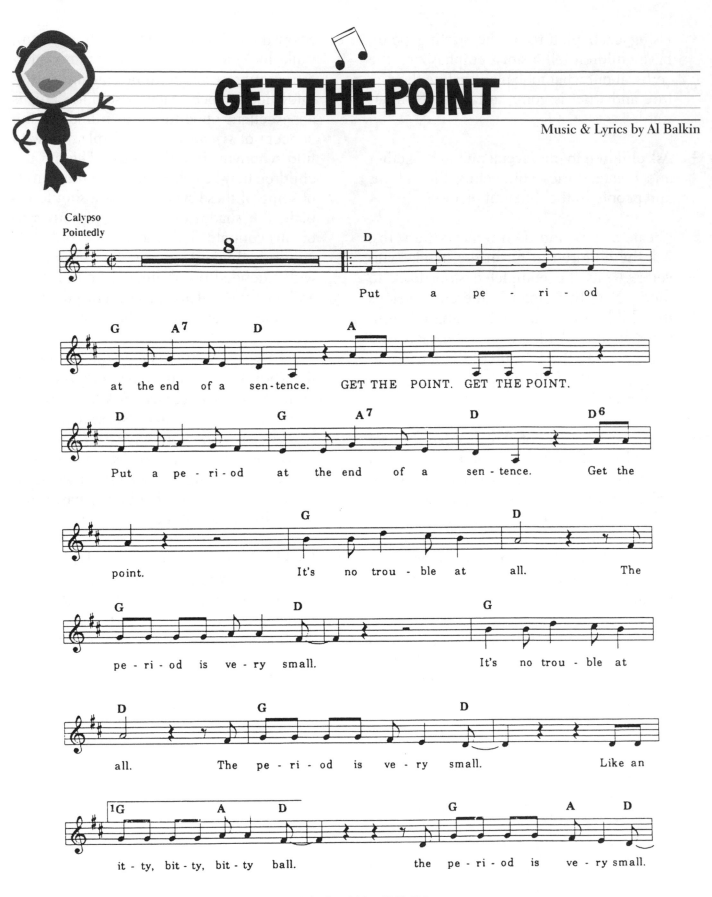

Calypso
Pointedly

D
Put a pe - ri - od

G **A7** **D** **A**
at the end of a sen - tence. GET THE POINT. GET THE POINT.

D **G** **A7** **D** **D6**
Put a pe - ri - od at the end of a sen - tence. Get the

G **D**
point. It's no trou - ble at all. The

G **D** **G**
pe - ri - od is ve - ry small. It's no trou - ble at

D **G** **D**
all. The pe - ri - od is ve - ry small. Like an

1 G **A** **D** **G** **A** **D**
it - ty, bit - ty, bit - ty ball. the pe - ri - od is ve - ry small.

*This song lends itself readily to 2-part harmony, particularly on the words: "It's no trouble at all. The period is very small."

LYRICS

Put a period at the end of a sentence.

Get the point. Get the point.

Put a period at the end of a sentence.

Get the point.

It's no trouble at all.

The period is very small.

It's no trouble at all.

The period is very small.

Like an itty, bitty, bitty ball, the period is very small.

Repeat.

Like an itty, bitty, bitty ball, the period is very small.

Like an itty, bitty, bitty ball, the period is very small.

The period is very small.

Repeat.

Very, very, very, very,

Very, very, very, very,

Very, very, very, very,

Very, very, very, very,

Very, very, ve–ry, ve—ry small.

Get the point.

ACTIVITIES

Without the number one punctuation mark—the period—words would run together like scrambled eggs and make no sense. This calypso song celebrates the period's existence. Children will learn the primary function of a period (to indicate the end of a sentence) and, through the constant pun on "point," what it looks like. The original title of this song was "Period Piece" (another pun); however, third-grade children in Chicago kept calling it "Get the Point." They won their point.

1. Ask the children to circle all the periods on a newspaper page, and then have each child report on the number of periods circled.

2. Read sentences, poems, or stories aloud, and replace each period with a sound, either vocal or instrumental (using a drum or some other rhythm instrument).

3. Use maps to find cities, which are indicated by a period-like dot. Stress how dots or points are important.

4. Point out that the word "period" has another important meaning relating to time (such as a period in history or a class period).

5. Create run-on sentences and rewrite them into separate sentences with periods.

6. Demonstrate with money and decimals the importance of little things, such as points. Show how simply moving a point can alter the value of a number (e.g., one dollar can become one hundred dollars).

7. Read a simple story aloud and have the children stand when they think there should be a period. (Pause slightly where the periods occur.)

8. Create a picture using only dots from a pencil point.

9. Show slides of great Impressionist paintings in which the artists used dots of color to create pictures of unusual light and beauty. Let the children try this technique.

10. Show the children the basic rhythms of calypso music by playing various percussion instruments, such as clavés, maracas, bongos, and guiro. (If you are in a school library, the music teacher usually has these instruments and might help you work with the children. If you are in a public library, you might be able to purchase these instruments or borrow them from a local school. If you have a synthesizer, you might be able to produce the sound of the steel drum, which is the most characteristic sound of authentic calypso music.)

11. Have children create their own rhythm instruments to accompany the song. Anything goes.

12. When the children say "Get the point," have them make periods in the air with their index fingers to punctuate (pardon the pun) each word. Reinforce their movements and words with percussion instruments.

13. Make up movements to go with the instrumental version. Ask volunteers to play the rhythm instruments along with the group's movements. Make sure that any child who wishes gets a chance to play the rhythm instruments.

14. Play several authentic calypso songs from the Caribbean Islands and tell the children more about calypso music. Explain its origins and discuss its similarities with other music. (In a sense, it's Caribbean rap with melodies.)

LETTERS TO SOUNDS

Music & Lyrics by Al Balkin

With spirit

Make a sound for the let-ter A. A, A, A, A, A.
Make a sound for the let-ter C. C, C, C, C, C.
Make a sound for the let-ter E. E, E, E, E, E.

Make a sound for the let-ter B. B, B, B, B, B.
Make a sound for the let-ter D. D, D, D, D, D.
Make a sound for the let-ter F. F, F, F, F, F.

Make a sound for the let-ter G. G, G, G, G, G.
Make a sound for the let-ter I. I, I, I, I, I.
Make a sound for the let-ter K. K, K, K, K, K.

Make a sound for the let-ter H. H, H, H, H, H.
Make a sound for the let-ter J. J, J, J, J, J.
Make a sound for the let-ter L. L, L, L, L, L.

Make a sound for the let-ter M. M, M, M, M, M.
Make a sound for the let-ter O. O, O, O, O, O.
Make a sound for the let-ter Q. Q, Q, Q, Q, Q.

Make a sound for the let-ter N. N, N, N, N, N.
Make a sound for the let-ter P. P, P, P, P, P.
Make a sound for the let-ter R. R, R, R, R, R.

Make a sound for the let-ter S. S, S, S, S, S.
Make a sound for the let-ter U. U, U, U, U, U.
Make a sound for the let-ter W. W, W, W_____

Make a sound for the let-ter T. T, T, T, T, T.
Make a sound for the let-ter V. V, V, V, V, V.
Make a sound for the let-ter X. X, X, X, X, X.

Make a sound for the let-ter Y. Y, Y, Y, Y, Y.

Make a sound for the let-ter Z. Z, Z, Z, Z, Z.

Ma-ny sounds in the al-pha-bet. We'll meet more, but not just yet.

From those sounds each word will grow. Ma-ny words we'll get to know.

Make a sound for the letter A.
A, A, A, A, A.

Make a sound for the letter B.
B, B, B, B, B.

Make a sound for the letter C.
C, C, C, C, C.

Make a sound for the letter D.
D, D, D, D, D.

Make a sound for the letter E.
E, E, E, E, E.

Make a sound for the letter F.
F, F, F, F, F.

Make a sound for the letter G.
G, G, G, G, G.

Make a sound for the letter H.
H, H, H, H, H.

Make a sound for the letter I.
I, I, I, I, I.

Make a sound for the letter J.
J, J, J, J, J.

Make a sound for the letter K.
K, K, K, K, K.

Make a sound for the letter L.
L, L, L, L, L.

Make a sound for the letter M.
M, M, M, M, M.

Make a sound for the letter N.
N, N, N, N, N.

Make a sound for the letter O.
O, O, O, O, O.

Make a sound for the letter P.
P, P, P, P, P.

Make a sound for the letter Q.
Q, Q, Q, Q, Q.

Make a sound for the letter R.
R, R, R, R, R.

Make a sound for the letter S.
S, S, S, S, S.

Make a sound for the letter T.
T, T, T, T, T.

Make a sound for the letter U.
U, U, U, U, U.

Make a sound for the letter V.
V, V, V, V, V.

Make a sound for the letter W.
W, W, W, W, W.

Make a sound for the letter X.
X, X, X, X, X.

Make a sound for the letter Y.
Y, Y, Y, Y, Y.

Make a sound for the letter Z.
Z, Z, Z, Z, Z.

Many sounds in the alphabet.

We'll meet more, but not just yet.

From those sounds each word will grow.

Many words we'll get to know.

ACTIVITIES

"Letters to Sounds" helps children become aware of speech sounds associated with each particular letter of the alphabet over and above the letter sound itself. Children will begin to see that letters are not isolated symbols; rather, when grouped together, letters are the basic building blocks for the actual sounds of words. The letters and their most common sounds are presented alphabetically.

1. Sing the song from A to Z with the actual letter sounds of the alphabet. This activity reinforces the order of the alphabet.

2. Sing the song again, this time using the sounds most typically applied to each consonant and vowel. Use the hard sound for consonants having both soft and hard sounds. Use the long vowel sound as in activity 1.

3. Repeat, using the soft consonant sounds (e.g., C and G) and the short vowel sounds.

4. Sing the song again using the instrumental version. For each letter, substitute one-syllable words that begin with that letter (e.g., "Make a word with the letter A. Ape, ape, ape, ape, ape."). Use long vowel sounds on all words. Consult the Rhyme-a-ton for help if needed.

5. Repeat activity 4 using short vowel sounds on all words.

6. Repeat activity 4, but pantomime the words. Assign children specific letters (those with harder letters will get easier ones when the activity is repeated). Give the children planning time and invite them to use any source that they might find in the room. Play the song and have the children fit their pantomimes into the flow. If a pantomime is not recognized immediately, it can be redone after the song so everyone has time to guess.

7. Repeat activity 6, but ask the children to create drawings, paintings, clay sculptures, or the like, using their assigned letters. Have them hold up their work as the song comes to their letter.

8. Repeat activity 6, but have the children cut out words or pictures from magazines. Be sure that the images are big enough to be seen by all. Have the children display their images as the song comes to their letter.

9. Divide the group into teams of four. Each child in a team will contribute one word. Each team will create a mini-story approximately two minutes long that includes the four words. All four words must be used at least twice, and the other teams must guess what those words are. You can make this a game in which each team gets points for determining the other teams' words. Most important, the activity demands acute listening. Teams might also find ways to involve the other teams (e.g., by having them make special sounds at certain places in the stories).

10. Using the instrumental version, sing, "Make a sound for the letter ___." Instead of singing the letter or a word, ask each child to invent a sound to fit into the flow of the song. The sound can be either vocal or nonvocal. Anything goes. The more unusual the better. Every child gets to make a sound when her or his letter comes up.

11. Repeat activity 10, but now everyone in the room is to make a vocal sound on the given letter at the same time. Again, the object is to make the strangest sound possible.

12. Play bingo using letter sounds. Make bingo cards with different letters of the alphabet on them. Say a letter sound and have the children mark their cards.

13. Do a letter sound search. Give each child a page from a newspaper. Assign the sounds and provide a set amount of time to find as many words as possible that contain those letter sounds. Ask the children to circle those words and count them.

WHAT'S A CONSONANT? WHAT'S A VOWEL?

Music & Lyrics by Al Balkin

WHAT'S A CON - SO - NANT? WHAT'S A VOW - EL? What is the dif - ference be -

tween them? It is ea - sy to tell the dif - ference once you've used and

seen them.

A con - so - nant can be al - most

a - ny let - ter you see. A con - so - nant can be al - most

a - ny let - ter you see ex - cept an A, or an I, or an

O, or a U, or an E

Those are the vow - els that con - so - nants

keep com - pa - ny.   *Repeat ad libitum till* 2.

LYRICS

What's a consonant?

What's a vowel?

What is the difference between them?

It is easy to tell the difference once you've used and seen them.

A consonant can be almost any letter you see.

A consonant can be almost any letter you see except an A, or an I, or an O, or a U, or an E.

Repeat.

Those are the vowels that consonants keep company.

Repeat ad libitum.

ACTIVITIES

A consonant can be almost any letter you see except an A, or an I, or an O, or a U, or an E. Those are the vowels that consonants keep company." These lines contain the basic message of "What's a Consonant? What's a Vowel?" and that message is exuberantly presented in the musical setting of an Irish jig. When children understand the differences between a vowel and a consonant, they will begin to apply their own problem-solving abilities to piece together the puzzle of written communication.

1. Make bingo cards having C or V on them. Call out different letters of the alphabet and let the children determine which are consonants and which are vowels. Repeat the game, but substitute letter sounds (short vowels) for the actual letters.

2. Have children add necessary vowels to complete vowelless words (e.g., "bt" could become bat, bet, bit, but; "ct" could become cat, cot, cut). Have the children make sentences with each word.

3. Repeat activity 2, but this time have children add consonants to complete words (e.g., "hu" could become hut, hum, hug). Have the children make sentences with the chosen words.

4. Take a sound such as "ed" and have children add whatever consonants are needed to make that sound into words (e.g., led, fed, bed). Use the Rhyme-a-ton for help. Have the children make sentences with the words.

5. Play Find the Consonant. Give each child part of a page from a magazine or newspaper. Allot a set amount of time to uncover specified consonants, for instance, all the Ts, Gs, and Hs. Repeat the procedure to play Find the Vowel. Let them try to beat the clock. Count the frequency of different letters to find the most "popular."

6. Sing a familiar song and leave out selected consonants and vowels. Repeat this procedure, but substitute different sounds for those eliminated. Let children correct the song.

7. Explore the world of people with hearing impairments by having the children wear earplugs as you talk, or by miming what you are saying, or by doing both. Let the children repeat what they think you said. Ask them what thoughts and feelings they had as a result of this experience. Also ask whether consonants or vowels were more difficult to identify without sound.

8. Ask why this song ends with E instead of alphabetically (with U) as in "Vowel Mambo." (Answer: The E rhymes with the Y in "company." Tell them a little about Y's versatility.)

9. Have children create word-picture books for both vowels and consonants. Using the books as departure points, the children can devise stories employing their own word collections.

10. Invite children to look around the room and identify objects beginning with consonants. Repeat the activity for objects beginning with vowels. Ask, "Are there more consonant or vowel beginnings?" The answer is obvious.

11. Play musical chairs with vowels and consonants. On consonants children keep moving, but on vowels they must sit down.

12. Starting on measure 17 ("consonant can"), hold up twelve-inch-square consonant letter cards on the first and fourth counts of each measure (strong beats).

    Start with B and end with T on measure 24. Switch to vowel cards at measure 25. Hold each card for a full measure.

    On repeat, when measure 17 resumes, hold up consonants V, W, X, Y, and Z for full measures. (That completes consonants.)

    At measure 25, repeat vowel choreography. Hold up all the vowels from measure 33 through each ending.

    Children holding consonant cards join in at measure 35 on "consonants" and hold those cards up together through both endings.

A SYLLABLE

Music & Lyrics by Al Balkin

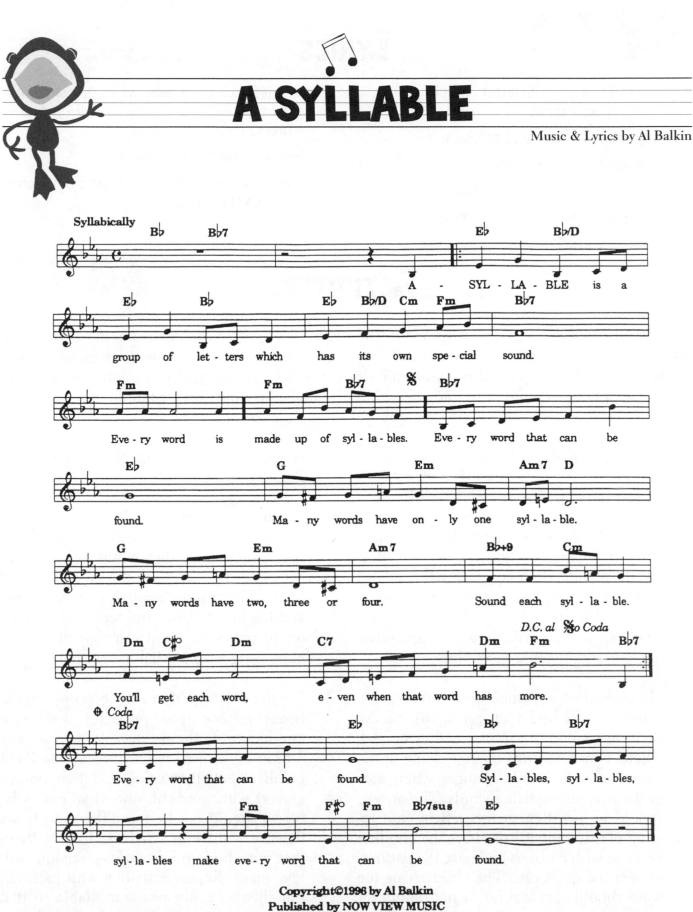

Syllabically

A - SYL - LA - BLE is a group of let - ters which has its own spe - cial sound.

Eve - ry word is made up of syl - la - bles. Eve - ry word that can be found.

Ma - ny words have on - ly one syl - la - ble.

Ma - ny words have two, three or four. Sound each syl - la - ble.

You'll get each word, e - ven when that word has more.

D.C. al Coda

⊕ *Coda*

Eve - ry word that can be found. Syl - la - bles, syl - la - bles,

syl - la - bles make eve - ry word that can be found.

LYRICS

A syllable is a group of letters which has its own special sound.

Every word is made up of syllables.

Every word that can be found.

Many words have only one syllable.

Many words have two, three, or four.

Sound each syllable.

You'll get each word, even when that word has more. *(Repeat till "found," and proceed to ending.)*

Every word that can be found.

Syllables, syllables, syllables make every word that can be found.

ACTIVITIES

Understanding the concept of *syllable* is the open sesame to sounding out almost any written word. Developing this ability allows a child to plunge confidently into the world of reading. "A Syllable" explicitly defines the concept, and the following suggestions and exercises are designed to explore, deepen, and solidify the child's understanding.

1. Emphasize that a syllable is always a single utterance with a beginning and an end. Have the children pretend to blow out the candles on a cake with a single quick breath. Explain that a syllable also takes just one breath. Practice this exercise: blow out the candle, then say a one-syllable word (e.g., play, read, learn, jump). Keep doing this exercise (blow/word, blow/word, blow/word, etc.). The syllable as a single utterance should become quite clear.

2. Have children continue to say one-syllable words (the Rhyme-a-ton can help) and ask them to look in the mirror as they do. Ask whether their mouths change shape or the sound of their words changes when they pronounce one-syllable words. The answer should be no. Repeat the activity, but instead of using the mirror, have the children practice with partners and have the partners answer the questions. The child saying the word should also feel his or her mouth for

added confirmation of the nonchanging shape.

3. Say two- and three-syllable words for the children to repeat. Follow the same basic procedures with a mirror and partners as in activity 2, but this time the answer should be yes. The mouth definitely changes shape, and the lips, tongue, and teeth get into different positions. Point out that the sound also changes from syllable to syllable.

4. Put the words used in activity 3 on a chalkboard or overhead projector and have children write them down. Repeat activity 3 from the written words themselves. Point out that if both their voices and their mouths change with words of more than one syllable, it should not be too difficult to break down a word into syllables. Inform them that with this understanding, reading will take place. Repeat activity 4 with partners, but silently. Limit words available so that

each partner has a good chance of determining the number of syllables, and hopefully the word itself, by sight alone.

5. Have children translate one-, two-, or multi-syllable words into body motions that reinforce the division of syllables.

6. Ask children to choose some typical athletic skills, such as hitting a baseball, throwing a basketball, catching a football, or swimming. Have them do these actions in slow motion and decide which are one, two, or more syllables. Make it clear that these movements can be broken down into their components just like words can be broken down into syllables.

7. Make up several word cards in various categories (e.g., animals, vehicles, places). Cut each word into syllables and place the pieces on the floor randomly so that no words are obvious. Let the children find syllables that go together to make words (e.g., el-e-phant,

ti-ger, li-on, gi-raffe, go-ril-la). If desired, assign children to teams for this task and give a prize for the team that finds the most words in the allotted time.

8. Have children explore the Rhyme-a-ton to find one-syllable words that could combine with other one-syllable words to form two-syllable words. Introduce the concept of *compound word*.

9. Using examples, point out that almost every syllable has at least one vowel, that a single vowel is often a syllable by itself (frequently at word beginnings), and that two consecutive consonants that are the same are usually broken up (though not in gi-raffe) so that the second consonant becomes the first letter of the next syllable (as in run-ning, hum-ming, diz-zy, dad-dy).

10. Play "I'm part of a word. Where's the rest of me?" (e.g., TI-ger, BRO-ther, SIS-ter, PA-per).

SOUNDS TO WORDS

Music & Lyrics by Al Balkin

Gospel feel

A, A, ap-ple. A, A,
C, C, cra-dle. C, C,

at. B, B, ba-by. B, B,
clay. D, D, doc-tor. D, D,

bat. E, E, ef-fort. E, E,
day.

end. F, F, fo-cus. F, F,

friend. G, G, gar-den. G, G,
I, I, im-age. I, I,

glide. H, H, help-ful. H, H,
inks. J, J, jus-tice. J, J,

hide. K, K, kitch-en. K, K,
jinx.

kite. L, L, lan-guage. L, L,

light. M, M, mo-tor. M, M,
O, O, op-era. O, O,

LYRICS

A, A, apple. A, A, at.

B, B, baby. B, B, bat.

C, C, cradle. C, C, clay.

D, D, doctor. D, D, day.

E, E, effort. E, E, end.

F, F, focus. F, F, friend.

G, G, garden. G, G, glide.

H, H, helpful. H, H, hide.

I, I, image. I, I, ink.

J, J, justice. J, J, jinx.

K, K, kitchen. K, K, kite.

L, L, language. L, L, light.

M, M, motor. M, M, met.

N, N, noodle. N, N, net.

O, O, opera. O, O, odd.

P, P, person. P, P, pod.

Q, Q, question. Q, Q, quake.

R, R, reading. R, R, rake.

S, S, sailing. S, S, stop.

T, T, trying. T, T, top.

U, U, under. U, U, undo.

V, V, victory. V, V, voodoo.

W, W, wonder. W, W, west.

X, X, x-ray. X needs rest.

Y, Y, yearning. Y, Y, you.

Z, Z, zebra. Z, Z, zoo.

Every letter we've gone through.

Sound all initial letters, both consonants and vowels, according to word usage, not letter name.

ACTIVITIES

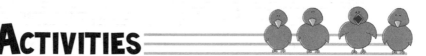

All the experiences with the alphabet, long and short vowels, consonants, letters to sounds, and especially syllables now come to fruition as all kinds of sounds become the springboard for all kinds of words. Knowledge of and practice with this concept are at the core of learning to read effectively.

1. After singing "Sounds to Words" while following each word on a large visual aid, have each child make up a sentence for each word in the song (e.g., "My favorite fruit is an *apple*." "Somebody is *at* the door."). Have the children present their sentences in pantomime, then aloud.

2. Ask groups of three or four children to create short stories using at least four words from the song. Have the children present their stories in pantomime, then aloud.

Have them draw or paint pictures of their stories.

3. Invite the children to substitute new words for every word in the song. Exchange long vowel sounds for words with short vowels and vice versa. Write the new words on a chalkboard or overhead projector. Divide each word into syllables. Using the instrumental accompaniment, sing the new words.

4. Repeat activities 1 and 2 with the new words from activity 3.

5. On a map of the United States, point out each state to the children. Have them repeat the state name after you, and ask them to supply the first two letters and possibly the last one from the sound. After each exercise, put that state on the screen or chalkboard.

6. Put all the states on the screen or chalkboard alphabetically, but in groups based on their beginning letter sounds (Alabama, Alaska, Arizona, Arkansas, California, Colorado, etc.).

> Question: Which first sound/letter begins the most state names?
>
> Answer: M and N are tied with eight each.
>
> Question: What first letters are not represented at all in the fifty state names?
>
> Answer: B, E, J, Q, X, Y, and Z.
>
> Question: How many first letters are represented?
>
> Answer: Nineteen.

7. Repeat activity 6 (without the questions) using family members' names. Graph the frequency of different sounds related to first names (e.g., in a group of twenty-five children, four mothers' names begin with B, three with D, one with U, etc.). Repeat the activity using last names. Repeat using the names of pets.

8. Take a sound (and word) such as "an" and have children list all the consonants they can add at the beginning to make new words (*an:* fan, tan, man, ran). Replace the *a* with a *u* (*un:* fun, run, sun, pun). Use the Rhyme-a-ton for help.

9. Point out that certain letters in the song have both hard and soft sounds. For instance, the hard *c* sound in "cradle" can become the soft *c* sound (like *s*) in "justice." Try to find other words with the soft *c* sound, such as "certain" or "celery." The same applies to *g*. Instead of the hard *g* in "garden," there is the soft *g* (like *j*) of "ginger" or "gypsy." Find more words with the soft *g*.

10. Help the children discover that the sound of a vowel letter name may often be the initial sound but only because it is combined with another letter and together they create the sound (e.g., *a* and *y* in "play"; *e* and *e* in "feel"; *e* and *a* in "real"; *o* and *a* in "foam"). Find words in the Rhyme-a-ton that have such combinations. Explore other combinations.

11. Point out that in many words, an *e* at the end creates the long vowel sound and that there is a consonant between the vowel and the *e* ending (e.g., home, ate, fuse, bite).

12. Explain that many words become completely different words by adding an *e* at the end (e.g., at + e = ate, us + e = use, bit + e = bite). Find more examples.

13. Have children begin a book of words that become other words by simply adding one letter. Encourage them to illustrate their words with pictures from magazines or with their own artistic creations.

NOUNSENSE

Music & Lyrics by Al Balkin

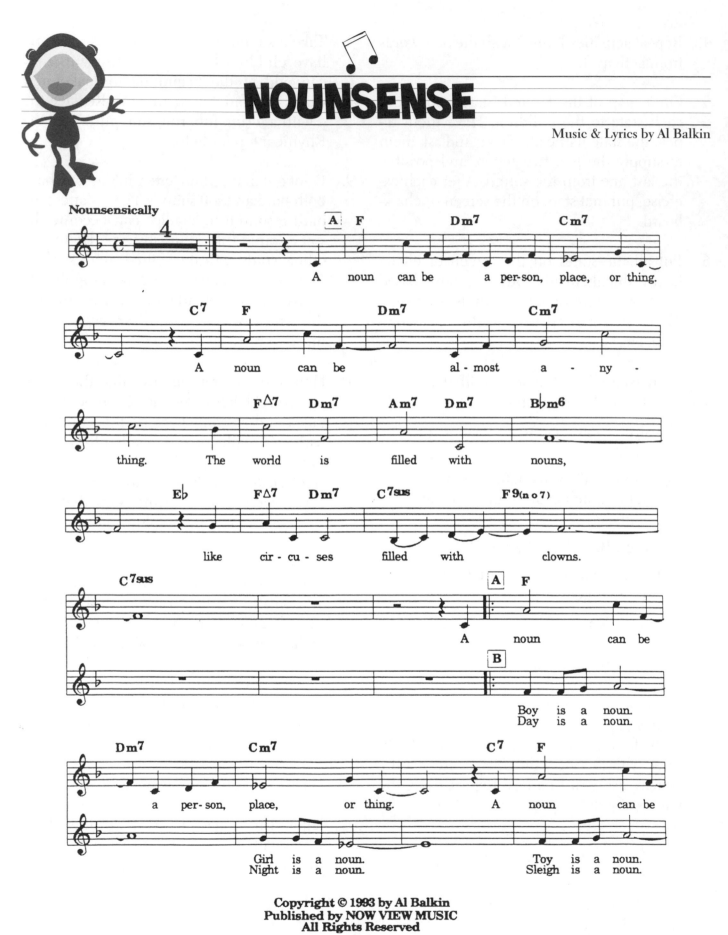

Nounsensically

A F Dm7 Cm7

A noun can be a per-son, place, or thing.

C7 F Dm7 Cm7

A noun can be al-most a - ny -

F△7 Dm7 Am7 Dm7 B♭m6

thing. The world is filled with nouns,

E♭ F△7 Dm7 C7sus F9(no7)

like cir - cu - ses filled with clowns.

C7sus

A F

A noun can be

B

Boy is a noun.
Day is a noun.

Dm7 Cm7 C7 F

a per-son, place, or thing. A noun can be

Girl is a noun.
Night is a noun.

Toy is a noun.
Sleigh is a noun.

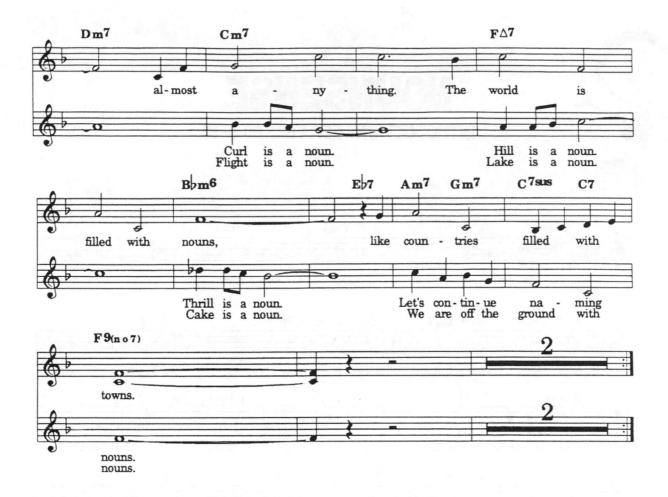

*B is sung for all verses. A is sung alone, then with the first, last, and other verses you choose. Add as many nouns in verse categories 3-10 as you wish. Make up new categories.

NOUNSENSE

INTRODUCTIONS FOR VERSES 3-10

Music & Lyrics by Al Balkin

LYRICS

A.   A noun can be a person, place, or thing.
     A noun can be almost anything.
     The world is filled with nouns,
     like circuses filled with clowns.

     A noun can be a person, place, or thing.
     A noun can be almost anything.
     The world is filled with nouns,
     like countries filled with towns.

B1. Boy is a noun. Girl is a noun.
     Toy is a noun. Curl is a noun.
     Hill is a noun. Thrill is a noun.
     Let's continue naming nouns.

B2. Day is a noun. Night is a noun.
     Sleigh is a noun. Flight is a noun.
     Lake is a noun. Cake is a noun.
     We are off the ground with nouns.

B is for all verses. A is sung alone first, then along with the first and last verse, or as many verses as desired. Add as many verse categories as you wish.

B3. Occupation nouns. Occupation nouns.
     Teacher's a noun. . . .

B4. Fruit nouns. Fruit nouns. Pick your fruit nouns.
     Peach is a noun. . . .

B5. Transportation nouns. Transportation nouns.
     Car is a noun. . . .

B6. Sports nouns. Sports nouns. Play your sports nouns.
     Baseball's a noun. . . .

B7. Vegetable nouns. Vegetable nouns.
     Carrot's a noun. . . .

B8. Find-your-place nouns. Find-your-place nouns.
     Ocean's a noun. . . .

B9. Animal nouns. Animal nouns.
     Lion's a noun. . . .

B10. Bird nouns. Bird nouns. Fly those bird nouns.
     Bluebird's a noun. . . .

Nouns are the basic building blocks of early language. With a limited noun vocabulary, young children can communicate most of their needs. Nouns are the foundation of sentences. The first section of "Nounsense" defines and amplifies the concept of *noun* as a "person, place, or thing." The remainder of the song (which if desired can be sung in harmony with the first section) develops that concept by providing numerous examples in a variety of categories. In these examples, nouns can also be the springboard for multidisciplinary learning. The children are invited to personalize and play with the song by contributing their own nouns in the various categories.

1. Play the first section of "Nounsense." It defines a noun. Ask children to look around the room, name whatever they see, and categorize it as a "person, place or thing."

2. Play the rest of the song with the children singing along and adding their own words in the various categories. This procedure will clarify and amplify their contributions in activity 1.

3. Tell the children that nouns were the words they used most often when they were babies. Ask them for examples of how babies and toddlers (perhaps their little brothers or sisters) use nouns to communicate their needs and wishes.

4. Read a story aloud from a book or newspaper but eliminate the nouns. Stop at the end of each sentence and ask children to supply the missing nouns. Accept any nouns that make sense and write the children's responses on the board or overhead projector. (Of course, their combined contributions will create quite a different story.) Read the original without stopping.

5. Play Nounball. Before a child can hit or kick the ball or run to a base, he or she must say a noun in a category selected for each inning (e.g., occupations, sports, transportation). For a warm-up, ask the children to supply nouns in the broader categories of persons, places, or things.

6. Prepare sets of noun flash cards. Shuffle the cards and then have the children reassemble them into sets (e.g., vegetables, fruits, locations).

7. Ask the children to create sentences using the following format:

   _____ [name of person]

   was sitting by _____ [location]

   while she [he] was eating _____ [food].

8. Read a story and let the children replace each noun with the name of its general category: person, place, or thing (e.g., farmer—person; city—place; desk—thing).

9. Have the children sing some familiar songs but replace all the nouns with hand claps (e.g., "Row, row, row your [clap] gently down the [clap]. Merrily, merrily, merrily, merrily, [clap] is but a [clap]."). Repeat this activity with nursery rhymes.

10. Play Find the Nouns by asking the children to circle all the nouns on a newspaper page.

Set a time limit and then count the number of nouns circled by each child. If desired, award a prize for the greatest number circled.

11. Plan a party. Have the children list as many nouns as possible to create a great party. Repeat this activity with nouns related to packing for a trip.

12. Using magazine pictures, make collages of nouns in various categories.

13. Have children create two-line poems about any noun they choose. The rhyme scheme will be *aa*. Try four-line poems with the rhyme scheme *abab*, *abcb*, or *aabb*. Use the Rhyme-a-ton for help. If you are in a school library, you might ask the music teacher to assist in setting the poems to music.

PRONOUNS

Music & Lyrics by Al Balkin

plumb - er_____ could be he

or she._____ Dan - cer or

den - tist, could be she

or he._____ Far - mer or

flo - rist, al - so she

or he. But on - ly he for

hus - band, she for wife. No choice

there. That is life.

Repeat A through 2)
then go to C

He for per - son.

She the same. It for what - e - ver

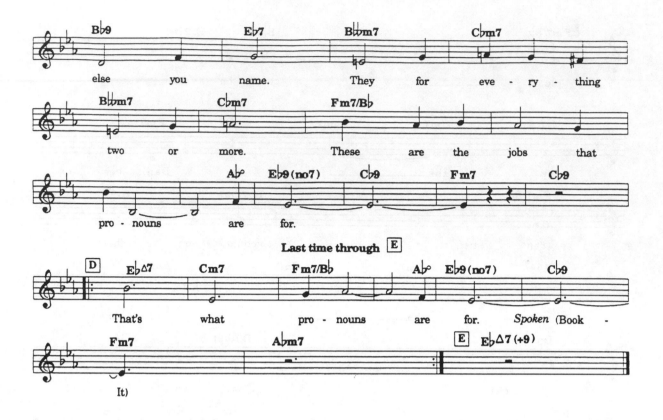

else you name. They for eve - ry - thing

two or more. These are the jobs that

pro - nouns are for.

Last time through

That's what pro - nouns are for. *Spoken* (Book -

It)

LYRICS

A. Pronouns stand for nouns.

That's the big job they can do.

Such as he, she, it, they, you—

Just to mention a few.

Pronouns stand for nouns.

We all use them every day.

Such as she, he, it, you, they—

Help us say what we say.

B. Pilot or plumber—could be he or she.

Dancer or dentist—could be she or he.

Farmer or florist, also she or he.

But only he for husband, she for wife.

No choice there. That is life.

Repeat A through ending 2, then go to C.

C. He for person. She the same.

It for whatever else you name.

They for everything two or more.

These are the jobs that pronouns are for.

Name different nouns such as "book" along with each equivalent pronoun, such as "it" for "book," "she" for "Mary," "he" for "Bob," "it" for "wall," "they" for "windows," and so on. After naming each pair, sing D.

D. That's what pronouns are for.

ACTIVITIES

Second only to nouns in importance and frequency are pronouns. In this song, children quickly learn that the primary function of pronouns is to take the place of nouns. By standing in for certain nouns, pronouns both minimize repetition and maximize the impact of the nouns they replace. This allows thoughts to flow more freely, naturally, and effectively. Understanding how, when, and why we use pronouns is a quantum leap in manipulating language. "Pronouns" gives children the opportunity to make that leap by providing numerous noun/pronoun matchups and encouraging them to offer their own examples. It also directs attention to other components of language construction and needed comprehension, specifically gender and number (singular/plural).

1. Play and perform the first section of "Pronouns," which succinctly defines the concept.

2. Play and perform the second section, which gives several noun/pronoun matchups.

3. Substitute different occupations for those listed and repeat activity 2.

4. Play and perform the third section, which solidifies male-female gender and introduces the neuter "it" along with the plural "they," standing for "everything two or more." Explain that in English there is no special plural pronoun for persons and that all genders are lumped together under the generic "they." It might be fun to hear the children's reasons for this.

5. Play and perform the fourth section ("That's what pronouns are for.") until the children run out of ideas.

6. Play Guess That Noun. Ask children to supply pronouns for and descriptions of the nouns they have in mind. Here are some examples:

   "*I* write books. *I* am an [author]."

   "*She* assists the surgeon in the operating room. *She* is either a [doctor] or a [nurse]."

   "*It* shines light on the earth at night. *It* is the [moon]."

   "*They* used to pull wagon trains across this country. *They* are [oxen]."

   This would make a good team game.

7. As you read a story, substitute pronouns for all the nouns. Then have the children replace the pronouns with nouns. Be prepared for a different story than the one you just read. Write the children's nouns on a chalkboard or overhead projector. After all the nouns are replaced, read the new story. Ask the children which story they like better and why.

8. Sing some familiar songs replacing nouns with pronouns. Have the children put back the nouns.

9. "Pronouns" does not give examples of every pronoun used in English. Ask children to add some that are missing from the song. List the most common ones, such as "me," "her," "him," "them," "we," "us," "that," "these," and "those." Explain that there are still more that have special functions (such as "who," "what," etc.), but for now, those listed in the song and in this activity will suffice.

10. Give each child a newspaper or magazine page. Have the children circle all the pronouns they can find on their page. Ask them to identify the correct noun for each pronoun they find.

11. Show pictures with multiple objects in them and ask the children to substitute appropriate pronouns for the objects (nouns) they see.

12. Give each child a picture as story starter. Ask the children to write stories (they can do this in pairs), first with nouns only, then using both nouns and pronouns. Ask them which version they prefer. Remind them that the pronouns must be logically connected to their noun "parents." Have the children exchange stories for editing, then give the stories back to their original authors for rewriting and reading aloud.

ONE COMPLETE THOUGHT

Music & Lyrics by Al Balkin

Happily

Chorus

ONE COM-PLETE THOUGHT.

One com-plete thought. A sen-tence con-tains at least one com-plete thought.

One com-plete thought.

Verse

One com-plete thought.
One com-plete thought.

A
1.Birds are sing-ing. One com-plete thought.
2.Let's go run-ning. One com-plete thought.

One com-plete thought. One com-plete thought. Spring is spring-ing.
One com-plete thought. One com-plete thought. Sum-mer's co-ming.

One com-plete thought. A sen-tence con-tains at least one com-plete thought.
One com-plete thought.

Verse

Chorus
(after every 2 verses)

B
1.Clean the store. One com-plete thought.
2.Trees are tall. One com-plete thought.

Shine the door. One com-plete thought. Scrub the floor.
Leaves are small. One com-plete thought. See them all.

One com-plete thought. A sen-tence con-tains at least one com-plete thought.

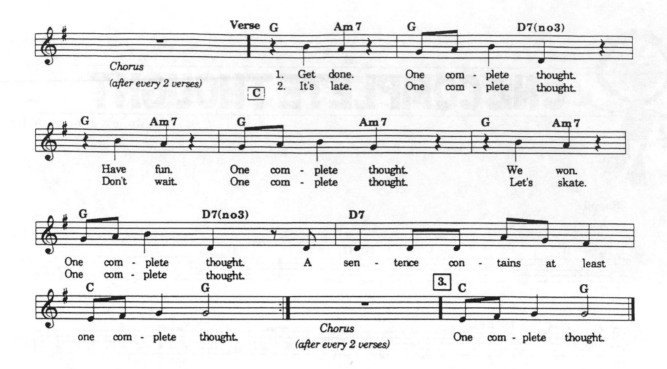

*Add own 4-syllable sentences to **A**; 3-syllable sentences to **B**; 2-syllable sentences to **C**.

LYRICS

CHORUS

    One complete thought.

    One complete thought.

    A sentence contains at least one complete thought.

    One complete thought.

Repeat chorus.

A1. Birds are singing.

    One complete thought.

    One complete thought.

    One complete thought.

    Spring is springing.

    One complete thought.

    A sentence contains at least one complete thought.

A2. Let's go running.

    One complete thought.

    One complete thought.

    One complete thought.

    Summer's coming.

    One complete thought.

    A sentence contains at least one complete thought.

Repeat chorus.

B1. Clean the store.

    One complete thought.

    Shine the door.

    One complete thought.

    Scrub the floor.

    One complete thought.

    A sentence contains at least one complete thought.

B2. Trees are tall.

    One complete thought.

    Leaves are small.

    One complete thought.

    See them all.

    One complete thought.

    A sentence contains at least one complete thought.

Repeat chorus.

C1. Get done.

    One complete thought.

    Have fun.

    One complete thought.

    We won.

    One complete thought.

    A sentence contains at least one complete thought.

C2. It's late.

    One complete thought.

    Don't wait.

    One complete thought.

    Let's skate.

    One complete thought.

    A sentence contains at least one complete thought.

Repeat chorus.

Add your own four-syllable sentences to A, three-syllable sentences to B, and two-syllable sentences to C.

What is a sentence other than a group of words starting with a capital letter and ending with a period? Do we define a sentence simply by that grammatical frame? How do we determine meaning? What gives sense to a sentence? This song emphatically states, "A sentence contains at least one complete thought." To clarify and strengthen that concept, the song offers short examples of both declarative and imperative sentences. Each short sentence represents "one complete thought." These sentences are constructed in four (section A), three (section B), and two (section C) syllables. Children are encouraged to create their own sentences in each of those syllable arrangements. After these experiences, children will more clearly understand what a sentence is in terms of function, construction, and, most important, meaning and sense.

1. Play the song one time through. Play it again, show the children the words, and ask them to sing the chorus. Play it a third time and have them not only join in at the chorus but sing all the "one complete thought" lines after each sentence.

2. Form two groups of children. Repeat the song with groups 1 and 2 both singing the chorus; however, only group 1 will sing the sentences and only group 2 will answer with the "one complete thought" responses. Reverse the groups and repeat the activity.

3. Repeat the song with everyone singing everything. Repeat, but pantomime the verses instead.

4. Repeat the song and have children stand as they sing "one complete thought" after every sentence and during each chorus. Have them hold up either hand to indicate the "one."

5. Form groups of four children each. Instruct them to create new four-syllable sentences for section A. Pantomime new verses to the instrumental accompaniment. Repeat this activity with three-syllable sentences for section B and two-syllable sentences for section C. Let children try to guess the pantomimes without stopping the music.

6. Repeat activity 5, but now ask the children to sing their new verses.

7. Ask, "Is 'one complete thought' a sentence?" If so, why? If not, why not? Explain that a sentence needs at least one subject and one verb. Much of the time it also needs an object. "One complete thought" is just a three-word phrase with no verb or object. Therefore it cannot be a sentence. *Explain that in a sentence the subject does the action of the verb, and the object receives the action.* Give a few examples such as the following:

   "She owns a dog." [She = subject; owns = verb; dog = object]

   "He saw the bird." [He = subject; saw = verb; bird = object]

   Ask the children for more examples.

8. Some sentences from the song do not appear to have a subject (e.g., "Clean the store," "Scrub the floor," "Get done," and "Have fun"). Explain that when a sentence

starts with a command verb (e.g., run, go, climb, jump), the subject is really "you." The "you" does not have to be said or written because it is understood. Such groups of words are considered sentences because they have a subject and a verb. To solidify this concept, have children put a "you" in front of every imperative verb in the song.

9. Ask children to make up some imperative sentences. Insert them into the song where they fit and sing the new song.

10. Have children create sentence pictures using appropriate art materials. Before each child provides the meaning of her or his picture, let the group guess the sentences and point out the subject, verb, and possible object of each one. Repeat this activity using single images or groups of pictures from magazines, perhaps organized around a particular theme.

SINGULAR OR PLURAL

Music & Lyrics by Al Balkin

Choicefully

Chorus

SIN-GU-LAR OR PLU - RAL. Ea - sy to ex - plore.

Sin-gu-lar means just one, plu - ral means more.

Verse

1) Cloud sin-gu-lar. Clouds____ plu - ral.
2) Game sin-gu-lar. Games____ plu - ral.

House sin-gu-lar. Hou - ses plu - ral.
Prize sin-gu-lar.

2)

Pri - zes plu - ral. Plu - ral means

*Last time only

Chorus

more.

Note: See additional verses on page 61.

LYRICS

CHORUS

Singular or plural.

Easy to explore.

Singular means just one,

Plural means more.

1. Cloud singular. Clouds plural.

   House singular. Houses plural.

2. Game singular. Games plural.

   Prize singular. Prizes plural.

Repeat chorus.

3. Man singular. Men plural.

   Ox singular. Oxen plural.

4. Girl singular. Girls plural.

   Nurse singular. Nurses plural.

Repeat chorus.

5. Coat singular. Coats plural.

   Size singular. Sizes plural.

6. Wolf singular. Wolves plural.

   Bridge singular. Bridges plural.

Repeat chorus.

ACTIVITIES

The chorus sums up the concept with the simplicity it's due. The song then presents a number of nouns in their singular form and immediately follows each singular with its plural counterpart. This provides solid reinforcement for the norm and a frame of reference for the exception.

1. Play the song all the way through. Play it again and let the children join in the chorus each time. Have children now sing all the verses as well.

2. Help the children discover that most of the nouns merely add an *s* to the singular in order to make it plural (e.g., boy/s, girl/s, horse/s, boat/s). Show pictures of singular and plural nouns (e.g., dog/dogs) and have the children read and spell both forms.

3. Let the children individually create new verses, adding *s* for the plural. Present the new verses to the group and have the children sing the new verses.

4. Point out that singular nouns ending in *y* eliminate the *y* and substitute *ies* for the plural (e.g., "story" becomes "stories"). Help the children discover some more *y*-ending words.

5. Call children's attention to the change from "man" (singular) to "men" (plural) and from "wolf" (singular) to "wolves" (plural). Explain that many words do not follow the patterns shown in activities 3 and 4 for changing from singular to plural and that those words must be learned individually. Help children discover as many of these words as they can.

6. Have children create more new verses using all the different forms of plurals they have learned, and sing them accompanied by the instrumental recording. Show pictures of various nouns and have children identify which plural ending is required.

7. Play the Singular-Plural game. Have children put on blindfolds and guess the answers to such questions as the following: "Is there one person behind you? Two? Three? Are you hearing two, three, or four voices

singing? Are you hearing three boys and one girl? Four boys? Two girls and two boys? All girls? All boys?" This game will really enhance listening skills. The children are no longer dealing with just singular or plural. They are attempting to determine how many by listening.

8. Develop some musical games using bells, a piano, or other instruments capable of producing single tones. Ask the children how many bells are being sounded at the same time. How many piano keys? Play the bells or keys separately before playing them together. This way the children hear the "singular" first before the more complicated-sounding "plural."

9. Tell several stories of individuals who "singlehandedly" accomplished great things. Do the same for duos and for teams. Ask the children to contribute similar stories of people they might know or have heard about. Ask, "Is 'singlehanded' a good choice of words? Are there some things that can be accomplished by one person alone?" Have the group cite some specific examples (e.g., write a book, perform a play, sing a song, build a bookcase, bake a cake). Guide the children to discover that it often takes only one individual to initiate a project and to complete it. More often, it takes a team to realize the vision of a creative individual. Stress the crucial interrelationship between the individual and the group and the advantages of working together.

10. Explore the situation of the individual involved in a team sport. Which sports require the most awareness of and appreciation for the team's needs? Which sports require the least? Ask the children to imagine how participants in team sports might feel about the extraordinary accomplishments of certain individuals on their teams. Ask if any of the children have been in such a situation and want to share their experience.

11. All of activity 9 can easily apply to music, dance, and theater groups. Play some music by small jazz groups. Small jazz ensembles represent the perfect amalgam of individuals achieving both for themselves and for the group. The audience is the big winner.

12. Great people do stand out in history. Tell the children about individuals who changed their world, who inspired others, who were agents for good. Point out that even though these great people were human beings who sometimes made mistakes, those mistakes detracted not from their greatness but certainly from their "goodness." Also emphasize that great as these people were, they needed many others to help them achieve their destinies.

13. Point out that verbs must conform to singular and plural nouns (e.g., The diver rises. The divers rise. The girl runs. The girls run.). The verbs and nouns must be in agreement. Most commonly, the verb used with a singular noun adds an s. The opposite occurs with a plural noun. The noun adds the s instead of the verb. Nonagreement of verbs and nouns is a common error. Let the children make up sentences using single and plural nouns with their correct verb forms.

14. Explore the concept of *collective noun* (e.g., team, group, squad, flock). These nouns sound and look singular, but they mean more than one of some thing or person. At the same time, if you add an s to one of these words, it indicates more than one of that particular grouping (e.g., teams, groups, squads, flocks). Let children discover as many collective nouns as they can.

THE ADJECTIVE SONG

Music & Lyrics by Al Balkin

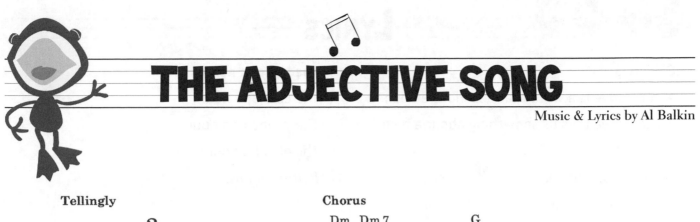

Tellingly

Chorus

Last time to Coda

An ad-jec-tive is a word that de-scribes a noun. An ad-jec-tive tells us some-thing a-bout a noun.

Verse

1. The co-lor of a noun. The shape of a noun. The size of a noun. The age of a noun. The smell of a noun. The taste of a noun. The feel of a noun. The ap-pe-al of a noun. An

2. The hap-py of a noun. The sad of a noun. The good of a noun. The bad of a noun. The hot of a noun. The cold of a noun. The young of a noun. The old of a noun. An

3. The ear-ly of a noun. The late of a noun. The crook-ed of a noun. The straight of a noun. The gen-tle of a noun. The mean of a noun. The ma-ny shades of in-be-tween-of-a noun-An-

Coda

And there are hun-dreds of ad-jec-tives to be found all a-round.

LYRICS

CHORUS

An adjective is a word that describes a noun.

An adjective tells us something about a noun.

The color of a noun.

The shape of a noun.

The size of a noun.

The age of a noun.

The smell of a noun.

The taste of a noun.

The feel of a noun.

The appeal of a noun.

Repeat chorus.

The happy of a noun.

The sad of a noun.

The good of a noun.

The bad of a noun.

The hot of a noun.

The cold of a noun.

The young of a noun.

The old of a noun.

Repeat chorus.

The early of a noun.

The late of a noun.

The crooked of a noun.

The straight of a noun.

The gentle of a noun.

The mean of a noun.

The many shades of in-between of a noun.

Repeat chorus.

And there are hundreds of adjectives to be found all around.

ACTIVITIES

This song, in a Middle Eastern musical style, clearly states the concept: "An adjective is a word that describes a noun." It then elaborates on how descriptions might include such characteristics as color, shape, size, age, smell, taste, feel, attitude, worth, and more. Adjectives bring nouns to life and differentiate between the same nouns (e.g., the tall man and the short man). Add a few more adjectives (the tall, lumbering, clumsy man and the short, swift, agile man) and you have a markedly more vivid description amplifying the difference between the same two nouns—man. Thoughtful use of adjectives will also accentuate the differences between different nouns (e.g., the tall man living in the small house). Through these two adjectives, the reader or listener forms a more accurate image of both the man and the house. This song offers opportunities to designate nouns and add adjectives that bring more meaning and life to the nouns. Always remember, however, what Mark Twain said: "When in doubt about using an adjective, leave it out." This is sage advice, but it should be applied judiciously. If a noun doesn't sufficiently conjure a clear picture of what the writer or speaker has in mind, a trip to the adjective store might be called for.

1. Conduct a quick word association test using a series of nouns (e.g., bridge, skyscraper, farm, cow, dog, house, car, plane, ship, sea). Such nouns have endless possibilities. They can even be separated into various categories. Ask the children to give their first adjective responses when they hear or see each noun (e.g., the red car, the huge ship, the rough sea).

2. Let children draw or paint a particular noun on poster paper. You may assign the nouns or they may choose their own. Display all the pictures around the room and ask the children to visit each picture and write any adjective they think is appropriate for that picture. If a child cannot spell the adjective well enough to make it sufficiently understandable, give her or him the correct spelling. After all the children have had an opportunity to visit each picture, discuss some of their adjective choices.

3. Give the group a list of adjectives and instruct them to draw or paint any noun that seems to go with a particular adjective. Invite children to share their nouns with the group.

4. Ask the children to cut out pictures from magazines, name the noun that their picture represents, and add an adjective that seems to go with it. Display the pictures around the room and discuss some particularly interesting or unusual contributions.

5. Assign one page of reading material to each member of the group. Have them circle every adjective. Discuss their choices.

6. Have children pantomime such adjectives as fast-slow/faster-slower, high-low/higher-lower, heavy-light/heavier-lighter, thin-thick/thinner-thicker, and so on. They may use any nouns they want to go with their adjectives.

7. Let the group play rhythm instruments to accompany the instrumental version of the song. Develop the song's Middle Eastern stylistic connection by relating it to the region itself and by playing recorded music from such countries as Israel, Saudi Arabia, Syria, and Egypt. Ask whether the children find a musical relationship between the songs.

8. Introduce the concept of *mode* (both musically and historically) other than major or minor. This song is in the dorian mode (D-D). Many songs are in pentatonic modes. Explain and illustrate these modes.

FACT OR FANTASY?

Music & Lyrics by Al Balkin

Note: See additional verses on page 67.

LYRICS

1. Fact or fantasy?
   Elephants can fly.
   Sounds like fantasy.
   Even if they try.

2. Fact or fantasy?
   Clouds can carry rain.
   Surely that's a fact.
   Someone can explain.
   CHORUS
   Fact or fantasy?
   Which one will it be?
   Fact or fantasy?
   Maybe we'll agree.

3. Fact or fantasy?
   Trees take years to grow.
   Surely that's a fact.
   One that we all know.

4. Fact or fantasy?
   Dogs can drive a train.
   Sounds like fantasy.
   Just consult your brain.
   Repeat chorus.

5. Fact or fantasy?
   Motorcycles float.
   Sounds like fantasy.
   Better go by boat.

6. Fact or fantasy?
   Hummingbirds are small.
   Surely that's a fact.
   Have you seen one tall?

CHORUS (WITH CODA)

   Fact or fantasy?
   Which one will it be?
   Fact or fantasy?
   Maybe we'll agree.
   Maybe we'll agree.

Add your own verses of fact or fantasy. Use coda only at end of all verses.

Second ending is used after the second of every two verses.

"Fact or Fantasy?" calls attention to the concept that some things are indisputably facts and others are indisputably fantasy. However, many fantasies are based on fact. They could not exist unless fact was supporting them. Sometimes fantasy becomes fact. Jules Verne, for example, wrote about going to the moon long before the actual event. Fantasies may use facts to help a story ring true, but the whole is still fantasy. Facts give credence to the fantasy. This is the basis for most fiction. If the facts didn't exist, the fantasy would be less believable. The possibility that "it could happen" gives a fantasy force. Facts can be manipulated to create a fantasy, and fantasy often involves facts.

1. Get acquainted with the song so you have a frame of reference for the concept of *fact or fantasy*.

2. Have children pantomime some facts and fantasies accompanied by the instrumental version. You can do the same.

3. Discuss books based on fact (such as *Roots*) and those based on fantasy (such as *Alice in Wonderland* or *The Hobbit*). Compare these fantasies with *The Wizard of Oz* (in which there are facts such as Kansas, a real dog, a tornado, and real people who take on new identities in a dream).

4. Discuss dreams as fantasies and ask for volunteers to share one of their dreams.

5. Separate fiction from fantasy by explaining their similarities and differences. Let the group know that a fantasy, as opposed to fiction, is most unlikely to happen in reality. A lot of fiction, however, is well within the realm of truth. Ask children to develop this idea from books they've read and TV shows or movies that they've seen. Explain that, in a sense, fantasy is extreme fiction. The film *Jurassic Park* is based on the fact that the dinosaur and other large extinct creatures did exist in prehistoric times. Their present-day reappearance, as far as we know scientifically, is pure fantasy. The human characters could exist quite easily, but the events they deal with could not.

6. Explain to children that once we enter and are absorbed in a fantasy world, that world, for us, may take on its own reality. We accept it for what it is. When that happens, we are hooked on the story. Ask children about stories, films, or TV shows that have drawn them into other worlds.

7. Have children draw or paint fantastic pictures.

8. Let children create pantomimes and mini-dramas based on facts. Do the same with fantasy.

9. Explain that in our real world, and in history, certain facts are so incomprehensible and inspiring (e.g., landing on the moon) that they sound like fiction. On the other hand, certain facts (e.g., the Holocaust, slavery) are so terrible and tragic that they are hard to believe. Ask children if they can give any examples of positive and negative facts that seem like fiction.

10. Let children make up some fantasy riddles that could actually happen, such as the following:

"Elephants can fly." [True, if they are in an airplane.]

"A dog could jump out of a plane at 25,000 feet without hurting himself." [True, if he were being held by a person wearing a parachute who had jumped out of the same plane.]

11. Discuss how most stories in newspapers are based on fact, but make it clear that the facts don't necessarily mean the truth and are often shaded by the reporter's opinion. Give the children an opportunity to develop the idea that the "facts" are different things to different people.

12. "Truth is stranger than fiction." Ask the children to find examples to support this statement.

13. Comic strips are fiction, but are often based on real life. Have children bring in their favorite comic strips and compare the strips' emphasis on fact, fiction, and fantasy.

14. Have children create their own scenarios for comic strips, based on either fact or fantasy. Let them develop ideas and dialogue along with proposed images. Provide art materials so the children can draw their comic strips, then display them in the room or around the library.

15. Invite children to move the way the instrumental version of "Fact or Fantasy?" tells them.

16. Play the instrumental version and ask the children, "What might you be seeing on the movie or television screen as this music is playing?"

17. Introduce the children to the Walt Disney classic *Fantasia*, which presents a variety of highly regarded orchestral music, much of it based on fantasy.

LEARN TO READ

Music & Lyrics by Al Balkin

Soft rock beat

READ, and you'll dis - co - ver. Learn to

read, and you will find there's a

world just out there wait - ing to fill your

heart and fill your mind. LEARN TO

READ,
2. and there's no end - ing to the
3. you'll have such plea - sure, though some -

world
times the sun will mix with rain. You will
E - ven

o - pen each door and win - dow, and cross each
so, each word's a trea - sure. The more you

Copyright © 1977, 1980, 1992 by Al Balkin
Published by NOW VIEW MUSIC

LYRICS

1. Learn to read, and you'll discover.
   Learn to read, and you will find
   There's a world just out there waiting
   To fill your heart and fill your mind.

2. Learn to read, and there's no ending
   To the world you'll get to know.
   You will open each door and window,
   And cross each bridge you need to grow.

3. Learn to read, you'll have such pleasure,
   Though sometimes the sun will mix with rain.
   Even so, each word's a treasure.
   The more you know, the more you'll gain.

4. Learn to read, you may find answers
   To some problems that bother you.
   When you read, there are no bound'ries.
   Your mind will do what it can do.

5. Learn to read. What's past is present.
   When you read, all time is now.
   Have yourself a great adventure,
   As you learn to read somehow.

ACTIVITIES

If ever there were any questions about the many values of reading, this highly motivational song seeks to answer them. "Learn to Read" and you will find there's a world out there just waiting "to fill your heart and fill your mind." The song has many applications, but most important, it expresses the joy of reading.

1. Stimulate a group discussion by asking such questions as these:

   "In your opinion, why is reading so important?"

   "What might we learn about the news from newspapers and magazines that we couldn't from television?"

2. Discuss the following lines from the song.

   "There's no ending to the world you'll get to know."

   "You'll have such pleasure, though sometimes the sun will mix with rain."

   "You may find answers to some problems that bother you."

   What kinds of problems might they be?

3. Have the children tell their thoughts about these words from the song: "What's past is present. When you read, all time is now."

4. Create stories about being in troublesome situations in which a lack of reading ability might put someone in more trouble—even danger.

5. Repeat activity 4, but this time explain how the ability to read well might get someone *out* of trouble or danger.

6. Assuming that reading is the most valuable skill one could acquire, what might be the second choice?

7. Discuss what the children read at home and how much time they spend doing it. Ask them to tell about the most recent book they read. Have them draw a picture of their favorite character from the book and tell the group why they chose that character. Ask what book they plan to read next.

8. Have the children set a goal for the number of books they plan to read. Using art and craft materials, have the children create their own Book Log. Include space for each child to record the titles, the number of pages in each book, the time it took to read each book, a few sentences describing what each book was about, and his or her personal opinion and recommendation. At a follow-up session, ask the children to share their Book Logs with the group.

STRETCH YOUR IMAGINATION

Music & Lyrics by Al Balkin

Tempo imaginato

1. The e - le - phant is sit - ting on his fav - or - ite chair. The ca - mel is comb - ing out his ca - mel's hair. The li - on is read - ing her li - on - bra - ry book. And the mon - key is learn - ing how to mon - key - wave bum - ble cook.

2. The cow is sing - ing a cow - try tune. The whale is eat - ing with a big soup spoon. The dol - phin is climb - ing a dol - phin ber - ry tree. And the pig is ri - ding pig - gie back on a bum - ble bee.

Chorus

STRETCH YOUR I - MA - GI - NA - TION. Let the "what ifs" flow. STRETCH YOUR I - MA - GI - NA - TION. Let it

grow... and grow... and grow... and grow. Let your i - ma - gi - na - tion grow.———

The   3. The di - no - saur is talk - ing on the di - no - phone. The

cro - co - dile is play - ing a slide trom - bone. The ti - ger is an - noun - cing the

ti - ger - vi - sion news. And the bear is wear - ing her bears - ket - ball shoes.

Chorus

STRETCH YOUR I - MA - GI - NA-TION. Let the "what ifs" flow.

STRETCH YOUR I - MA - GI - NA - TION. Let it grow... and grow... and

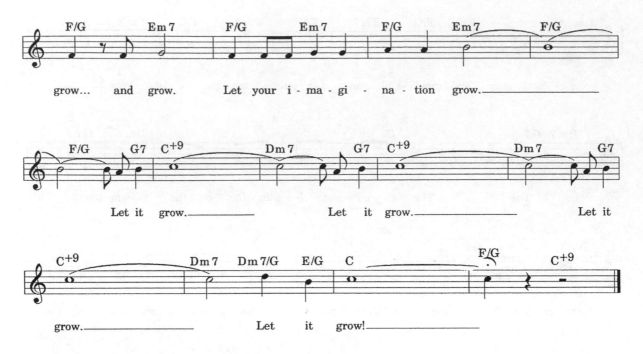

grow... and grow. Let your i - ma - gi - na - tion grow._____

Let it grow._____ Let it grow._____ Let it

grow._____ Let it grow!_____

* Add new verses (i.e. "The house is reading a houstory book.
The mouse is writing a moustery book". "The ant is becoming an
antelope. And the can is turning into a cantaloupe".)

Dedicated to **TYLER RAE BALKIN** , February 17, 1993 (age-8 months)

LYRICS

1. The elephant is sitting on his favorite chair.

   The camel is combing out his camel's hair.

   The lion is reading her lionbrary book.

   And the monkey is learning how to monkey-wave cook.

CHORUS

   Stretch your imagination.

   Let the "what ifs" flow.

   Stretch your imagination.

   Let it grow, and grow, and grow, and grow.

   Let your imagination grow.

2. The cow is singing a cow-try tune.

   The whale is eating with a big soup spoon.

   The dolphin is climbing a dolphin berry tree.

   And the pig is riding piggie back on a bumble bee.

Repeat chorus.

3. The dinosaur is talking on the dinophone.

   The crocodile is playing a slide trombone.

   The tiger is announcing the tigervision news.

   And the bear is wearing her bearsketball shoes.

Repeat chorus.

   Let it grow.

   Let it grow.

   Let it grow.

   Let it grow!

Add new verses (e.g., "The house is reading a houstory book. The mouse is writing a moustery book. The ant is becoming an antelope. And the can is turning into a cantaloupe.").

ACTIVITIES

Often lost in the pursuit of literacy skills is the cultivation of imagination and creativity. This song encourages children to expand their thinking: "Stretch your imagination. / Let the 'what ifs' flow. / Stretch your imagination. / Let it grow, and grow, and grow, and grow. / Let your imagination grow." The song makes its point with several silly but imaginative images (e.g., "The tiger is announcing the tigervision news. / And the bear is wearing her bearsketball shoes."). Is there any doubt that along with practical skills, outside-the-box thinking built our nation? Creativity and imagination enhance all aspects of language. Unlikely combinations bring greater possibilities, insights, and vision to reading, writing, and speaking. Stretch your imagination. Let it happen!

1. Have the children choose any images from the song that they would like to illustrate. Provide materials and let them try any medium that appeals to them. They may also create their own medium and be as crazy as they want.

2. Ask the children to create a completely new image in their mind and share it with the group. Provide materials so they can make a model or picture of it as in activity 1.

3. Form small groups and have each group create a story that stretches the imagination as far as it will go. Ask each group to share its story.

4. Ask the children to think about and pantomime an event that actually happened but seemed impossible at the time (e.g., walking on the moon).

5. Have the children create a story that they would like to see happen. Then have them create one that they would not like to see happen.

6. Share some examples of movies or TV shows that, in your opinion, were definitely "outside the box." Ask the children to contribute examples and have them tell why their choices are outside the box.

7. Have the children create new words and define them.

8. Ask the children to name the funniest movie they have ever seen and tell why it was so funny. Then have them name the scariest. Why? The saddest. Why? The happiest. And, of course—why?

9. Play several recordings of different kinds of music and ask the children which ones helped the most to stretch their imagination. Ask if their imagination stretches better without music.

10. Have each child tell the most creative thing she or he has ever done.

11. Ask "what if" questions and write the children's answers on poster paper.

BOOKS

Music & Lyrics by Al Balkin

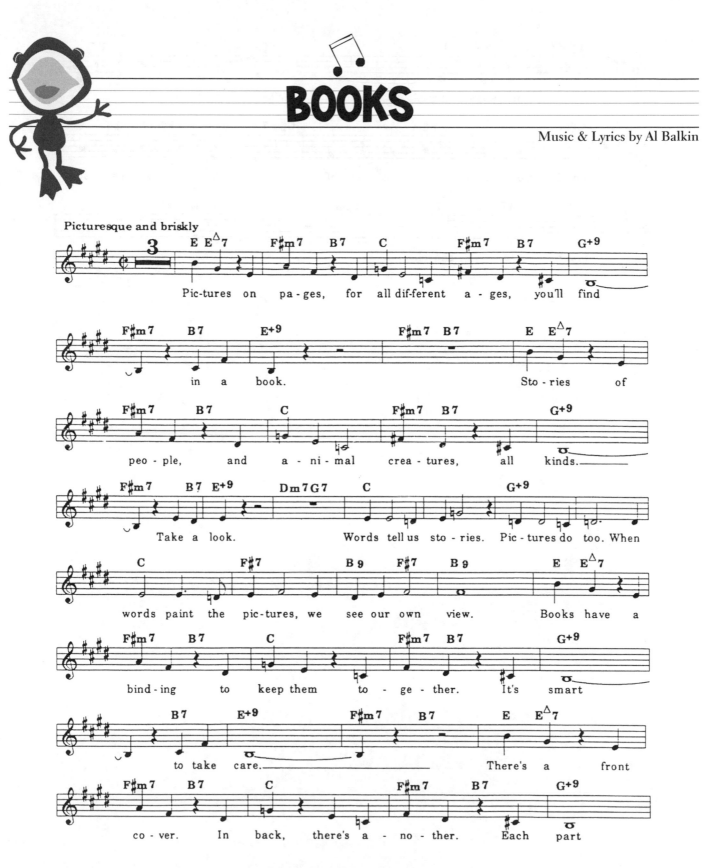

Picturesque and briskly

Pic-tures on pa - ges, for all dif-ferent a - ges, you'll find

in a book. Sto - ries of

peo - ple, and a - ni - mal crea - tures, all kinds.

Take a look. Words tell us sto - ries. Pic - tures do too. When

words paint the pic - tures, we see our own view. Books have a

bind - ing to keep them to - ge - ther. It's smart

to take care. There's a front

co - ver. In back, there's a - no - ther. Each part

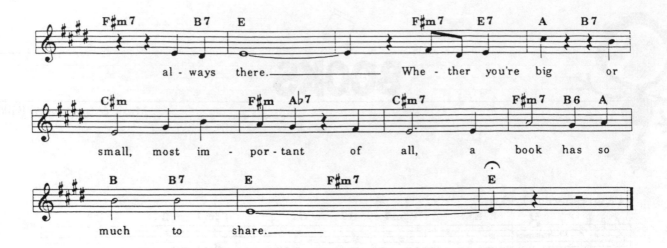

al - ways there.———— Whe - ther you're big or

small, most im - por - tant of all, a book has so

much to share.————

LYRICS

1. Pictures on pages,
   For all different ages,
   You'll find in a book.
   Stories of people,
   And animal creatures,
   All kinds. Take a look.

2. Words tell us stories.
   Pictures do too.
   When words paint the pictures,
   We see our own view.

3. Books have a binding
   To keep them together.
   It's smart to take care.
   There's a front cover.
   In back, there's another.
   Each part, always there.

4. Whether you're big or small,
   Most important of all,
   A book has so much to share.

ACTIVITIES

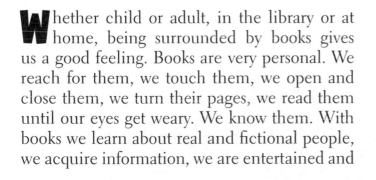

Whether child or adult, in the library or at home, being surrounded by books gives us a good feeling. Books are very personal. We reach for them, we touch them, we open and close them, we turn their pages, we read them until our eyes get weary. We know them. With books we learn about real and fictional people, we acquire information, we are entertained and sometimes even inspired. Books become life-long friends. It is often said that when you have a book to enjoy, you're never lonely. The song "Books" recognizes all this but also points out that a book has a physical presence of its own that we should be aware of and nurture. "It's smart to take care. . . . / A book has so much to share."

1. Listen to the song and discuss the lyrics before singing it. Using real books, show the children the physical characteristics and features mentioned in the song, such as the binding, the front and back covers, and the page setup as well as some things not mentioned, including the table of contents, the index, the title page, and so on. Show the children how to handle a book with care.

2. According to the song, "Words tell us stories. / Pictures do too." Have the children choose pictures from magazines or from pictures you provide and tell the stories that the pictures show.

3. According to the song, "When words paint the pictures, / We see our own view." Ask the children what this means to them.

4. Encourage children to tell experience stories to the whole group. Make the transition from telling the stories to writing them down. If the children have trouble making this transition, record their stories, write them down, and have the children copy

what you wrote. They can also play back their recorded stories and watch the written words.

5. Make a group book. Have each child write a page on a common theme and illustrate the page. The following are some examples of themes:

   "What I Do with My Friend"

   "My Favorite Sport"

   "What I Admire about a Special Person"

   "My Number One TV Show [Movie]"

   "A Trip into Town"

   Then have the children write individual storybooks.

6. Have the children make their own blank books by cutting writing paper and construction paper (for the covers) to a desired size and stapling them together. You might want to provide pre-cut paper for this activity. You can also pre-punch holes at the edges and have the children insert yarn or brads to hold the pages together.

7. Help children develop the journal-keeping habit. Give each child a blank book (or let them make one) and have them illustrate the covers. Have them write their first entry about making their journals and explain that they should set aside a few minutes each day to write in their journals.

8. Show the children a variety of ways to bind their books: stapling, tying with yarn, using small key rings, using a binding machine with plastic binders. If possible, include cloth binding.

9. Invite children to read their books to the group, then add the books to the library. Arrange for parents to hear this presentation by the group.

10. Cut pages and covers in the shape of a theme, such as a fish shape for an ecology program or a tulip shape for a spring program.

11. Demonstrate various techniques used by book illustrators and have the children practice these techniques. Invite a local illustrator to show her or his work to the children.

RHYME-A-TON
A Rhyming Dictionary of One-Syllable Words and Word Games for Children

The Rhyme-a-ton is a rhyming dictionary of one-syllable words children will likely encounter through speaking, listening, and reading. The Rhyme-a-ton will be most helpful with such obvious rhyming participation songs from *Tune Up to Literacy* as "Sing a Simple Rhyme." It will also be valuable with many other songs and activities in the program and will have an important place of its own in each child's growing library.

The greatest songwriters and poets cheerfully admit to using a rhyming dictionary. It is one of the basic tools of such creation, the others being the dictionary and the thesaurus. It is to the rhymesmith what nails are to the carpenter—indispensable. Most important, the Rhyme-a-ton, along with its special fun-filled word games, not only aids rhyme construction and builds vocabulary but also sparks ideas, expands imaginations, and stimulates the creative process. Adults and children alike will invent their own challenging Rhyme-a-ton experiences. Happy rhyming!

AB	ACE	ACK	
blab	ace	back	shack
cab	base	black	snack
crab	bass	clack	stack
dab	brace	crack	tack
drab	case	hack	track
gab	chase	jack	wrack
grab	face	Jack	yak
jab	grace	knack	
lab	lace	lack	**ACT**
nab	mace	Mac	act
scab	pace	pack	fact
slab	place	quack	pact
stab	race	rack	tact
tab	space	sac	
	trace	sack	

AD

ad
add
bad
Brad
cad
clad
dad
fad
glad
had
lad
mad
pad
plaid
sad

ADE

aid
blade
braid
fade
frayed (*and past of verbs in AY, such as prayed, weighed*)
glade
grade
jade
made
maid
paid
raid
shade
spade
suede
they'd
trade
wade

AFF

calf
chaff
gaff
graph
half
laugh
staff

AFT

aft
craft
daft
draft
graft
laughed
raft
shaft

AG

bag
brag
crag
drag
flag
gag
hag
jag
lag
nag
rag
sag
shag
snag
tag
wag

AGE

age
cage
gage
gauge
page
rage
sage
stage
wage

AIL

ail
bail
bale
brail
Braille
Dale
fail
flail
frail
Gail
gale
grail
hail
hale
jail
mail
male
nail
pail
pale
quail
rail
sail
sale
scale
shale
snail

stale
tail
tale
they'll
trail
vale
veil
wail
whale
Yale

AIN

bane
brain
cane
chain
crane
Dane
drain
feign
gain
grain
Jane
lane
main
Maine
mane
pain
pane
plain
plane
rain
reign
sane
Seine
Shane
slain
Spain
sprain

stain
strain
train
vain
vane
vein

AKE

ache
bake
Blake
brake
break
cake
drake
flake
Jake
lake
make
quake
rake
sake
shake
snake
stake
steak
take
wake

AL

Al
Hal
pal
Sal
shall

ALK

balk
caulk
chalk
gawk
hawk
squawk
stalk
talk
walk

ALL

all
awl
ball
bawl
brawl
call
crawl
drawl
fall
gall
hall
haul
mall
maul
pall
Paul
Saul
scrawl
shawl
small
sprawl
squall
stall
tall
thrall
trawl
wall

ALM

alm
balm
calm
Guam
palm
psalm
qualm

ALT

fault
halt
malt
salt
vault

AM

am
clam
cram
dam
dram
gram
ham
jam
jamb
lam
lamb
ma'am
Pam
pram
ram
Sam
scram
sham
slam
swam
tram
wham
yam

AME

aim
blame
came
claim
dame
fame
flame
frame
game
lame
maim
Mame
name
same
shame
tame

AMP

amp
camp
champ
clamp
cramp
damp
lamp
ramp
scamp
stamp
tamp
tramp
vamp

AN

an
Ann
Anne
ban
bran

can
clan
Dan
fan
Fran
Jan
Klan
man
Nan
pan
Pan
plan
ran
scan
span
tan
than
van

ANCE

chance
dance
France
glance
lance
Lance
pants
prance
stance
trance

AND

and
band
bland
brand
gland
grand
hand

land
sand
stand
strand

ANG

bang
clang
fang
gang
hang
pang
rang
sang
slang
sprang
tang
twang

ANGE

change
grange
mange
range
strange

ANK

bank
blank
clank
crank
dank
drank
flank
franc
frank
Frank
Hank
plank

prank
rank
sank
shank
shrank
swank
tank
thank
yank
Yank

ANT

ant
aunt
can't
chant
grant
Grant
pant
plant
rant
scant
slant

AP

cap
chap
clap
flap
gap
lap
map
nap
pap
rap
sap
scrap
slap

snap
strap
tap
trap
wrap
yap

APE

ape
cape
crepe
drape
gape
grape
nape
scrape
shape
tape

AR

are
bar
car
char
czar
far
jar
mar
par
R
scar
spar
star
tar
tsar

ARCH

arch

march
March
parch
starch

ARD

bard
barred
card
guard
hard
lard
yard

ARE

air
bare
bear
blare
care
chair
Claire
dare
ere
err
fair
fare
flair
flare
hair
hare
heir
lair
mare
mayor
pair
pare
pear

Pierre
prayer
rare
scare
share
spare
square
stair
stare
swear
tear
there
their
they're
ware
wear
where

ARGE

barge
charge
large
Marge
sarge

ARK

arc
ark
bark
Clark
dark
hark
lark
mark
Mark
park
shark
spark
stark

ARM

arm
charm
farm
harm

ART

art
Art
Bart
cart
carte
chart
dart
heart
part
smart
start
tart

ASH

ash
bash
brash
cache
cash
clash
crash
dash
flash
gash
gnash
hash
lash
mash
rash
sash
slash

smash
splash
thrash
trash

ASK

ask
bask
Basque
cask
flask
mask
task

ASP

asp
clasp
gasp
rasp

ASS

bass
brass
class
crass
gas
glass
grass
lass
mass
pass

AST

blast
cast
caste
fast
last

mast
past
vast

ASTE

baste
chased *(and
past of verbs in
ACE)*
haste
paste
taste
waist
waste

AT

at
bat
brat
cat
chat
fat
flat
gnat
hat
mat
Matt
Nat
pat
Pat
plat
Platte
sat
slat
spat
that
vat

ATCH

batch
catch
hatch
latch
match
patch
scratch
snatch
thatch

ATE

ate
bait
crate
date
eight
fate
fete
freight
gait
gate
grate
great
hate
Kate
late
mate
Nate
pate
plait
plate
rate
skate
slate
state
straight
strait
trait

wait
weight

ATH

bath
hath
math
path
wrath

AUNCH

haunch
launch
paunch
staunch

AUNT

aunt
daunt
flaunt
gaunt
haunt
jaunt
taunt
vaunt
want

AVE

brave
cave
crave
Dave
gave
grave
knave
rave
save
shave

slave
stave
they've
waive
wave

AW

aw
awe
daw
craw
draw
flaw
gnaw
haw
jaw
law
maw
paw
saw
thaw

AWN

brawn
dawn
drawn
faun
fawn
gone
lawn
pawn
Sean
yawn

AX

ax
flax
lax

Max
sax
tax
wax

AY

A
bay
bray
clay
day
eh
Fay
fray
gay
grey
hay
hey
J
jay
K
Kay
lay
lei
nay
neigh
pay
play
pray
prey
ray
Ray
re
say
slay
sleigh
spray
stay
stray
sway

they
tray
way
weigh

AZE

blaze
braise
chaise
craze
daze
faze
gaze
glaze
graze
haze
lays
laze
maze
phase
phrase
praise
raise
raze
rays (*add s to nouns and verbs ending in AY, such as plays, days*)

EACH

beach
bleach
breach
each
leech
peach
preach
reach
screech

speech
teach

EAK

beak
bleak
cheek
chic
clique
creak
creek
Creek
eek
eke
freak
Greek
leak
leek
meek
peak
peek
pique
reek
seek
sheik
shriek
sleek
sneak
speak
squeak
streak
teak
tweak
weak
week
wreak

EAL

deal

feel
heal
heel
he'll
keel
meal
Neal
Neil
peal
peel
real
reel
seal
she'll
squeal
steal
teal
veal
we'll
wheel
zeal

EAM

beam
cream
deem
dream
gleam
ream
scheme
scream
seam
seem
steam
stream
team
teem
theme

EAN

bean
clean
dean
Dean
Gene
glean
green
Jean
keen
lean
lien
mean
queen
preen
scene
screen
seen
sheen
spleen
teen
wean

EASE

cease
crease
fleece
geese
grease
Greece
lease
niece
peace
piece

EAST

beast
east
feast

fleeced
least
priest
yeast

EAT
beat
beet
bleat
cheat
eat
feat
feet
fleet
greet
heat
meat
meet
mete
neat
peat
Pete
pleat
seat
sheet
sleet
street
suite
sweet
treat
wheat

EAVE
cleave
eave
eve
Eve
grieve
heave

leave
peeve
sleeve
Steve
thieve
weave
we've

ECK
beck
check
Czech
deck
fleck
heck
neck
peck
speck
tech
trek
wreck

ED
bed
bled
bread
bred
dead
dread
Ed
fed
fled
Fred
head
Jed
lead
led
Ned
pled

read
red
said
shed
shred
sled
sped
spread
stead
Ted
thread
tread
wed

EE
be
bee
fee
flea
flee
free
gee
glee
he
key
knee
me
mi
plea
sea
see
she
ski
spree
tea
tee
ti
thee
three

we
ye

EED
bead
bleed
breed
cede
creed
deed
feed
freed
greed
heed
keyed
knead
lead
mead
need
plead
read
reed
seed
speed
steed
weed

EEP
cheap
cheep
creep
deep
heap
jeep
keep
leap
peep
reap
seep

sheep
sleep
steep
sweep
weep

EER
beer
bier
cheer
clear
dear
deer
ear
fear
gear
hear
here
jeer
leer
mere
near
peer
pier
queer
rear
sear
seer
sheer
smear
sneer
spear
sphere
steer
tear
tier
veer
year

89

EFT

cleft
deft
heft
left
theft

EG

beg
egg
keg
leg
Meg
peg
Peg

EL

bell
belle
cell
dell
dwell
fell
hell
jell
knell
Mel
Nell
quell
sell
shell
smell
spell
swell
tell
well
yell

ELT

belt
dealt
dwelt
felt
gelt
knelt
melt
pelt
svelte
veldt

EM

femme
gem
hem
M
phlegm
stem
them

EN

Ben
den
glen
Gwen
hen
ken
Ken
Len
men
N
pen
ten
then
when
wren
yen
Zen

ENCE

dense
fence
hence
pence
sense
tense
whence

ENCH

bench
clench
drench
French
quench
trench
wrench

END

bend
blend
end
fend
friend
lend
mend
send
spend
tend
trend
vend
wend

ENT

bent
Brent
cent
gent

Kent
Lent
meant
pent
rent
sent
spent
tent
Trent
vent
went

EP

pep
prep
rep
step
steppe

EPT

crept
kept
slept
stepped
swept
wept

ER

blur
bur
fir
fur
her
per
purr
sir
slur
spur

stir
were
whir

ERB

blurb
curb
herb
Herb
Serb
verb

ERGE

dirge
merge
purge
splurge
surge
urge
verge

ERSE

curse
hearse
nurse
purse
verse
worse

ERT

Bert
blurt
Burt
dirt
flirt
Gert
hurt
Kurt

pert
shirt
skirt
spurt
squirt

ERVE

curve
Irv
nerve
serve
swerve
verve

ESS

Bess
bless
chess
dress
guess
Jess
less
Les
mess
press
stress
Tess
tress
yes

EST

best
blest
chest
crest
dressed (and
past of verbs in
ESS)

guest
lest
nest
pest
quest
rest
test
vest
west
wrest
zest

ET

bet
debt
fret
jet
let
met
net
pet
set
sweat
threat
vet
wet
whet
yet

ETCH

fetch
retch
sketch
stretch
vetch
wretch

EW

blew
blue
boo
brew
chew
clue
coo
coup
crew
cue
dew
do
drew
due
ewe
few
flew
flu
flue
goo
grew
hue
Jew
knew
Lew
Lou
mew
moo
new
rue
shoe
shrew
stew
sue
Sue
threw
through
to

too
true
two
U
view
who
woo
zoo

EX

ex
checks (and add
s to nouns and
verbs in ECK)
flex
hex
Rex
specs
vex

IB

bib
crib
fib
glib
jib
rib

IBE

bribe
gibe
scribe
tribe

ICE

dice
ice
mice

nice
price
rice
slice
spice
splice
twice
vice

ICK

brick
chick
click
crick
flick
kick
lick
nick
Nick
pick
prick
quick
sic
sick
slick
stick
thick
tic
tick
trick
Vic
wick

ID

bid
did
grid
hid
kid

lid
mid
rid
skid
slid
squid

IDE

bride
Clyde
glide
guide
hide
pride
ride
side
slide
stride
tide
wide

IEF

beef
brief
chief
grief
leaf
reef
thief

IELD

field
healed (*and past
of verbs in EAL*)
shield
wield
yield

IF

cliff
if
miff
riff
skiff
sniff
stiff
tiff
whiff

IFT

drift
gift
lift
rift
shift
shrift
sift
sniffed (*and add
ed to verbs in IF*)
thrift

IG

big
brig
dig
fig
gig
jig
pig
rig
sprig
swig
twig
wig
Whig

IKE

bike
dike
hike
Ike
like
Mike
pike
psych
spike
strike
tyke

ILD

child
filed
mild
piled
smiled
styled
tiled
wild

ILE

aisle
bile
file
guile
I'll
isle
mile
pile
rile
smile
style
while
wile

ILL

bill
Bill
chill
dill
drill
fill
frill
Gil
gill
grill
hill
ill
kill
mill
Mill
nil
Phil
pill
quill
shrill
sill
skill
spill
still
thrill
till
trill
twill
will
Will

ILT

built
gilt
guilt
hilt
jilt
kilt

lilt
quilt
stilt
tilt
wilt

IM

brim
dim
grim
Grimm
gym
him
hymn
Jim
Kim
limb
prim
rim
skim
swim
Tim
trim
vim
whim

IME

chime
climb
crime
dime
grime
I'm
lime
mime
prime
rhyme
slime
time

IMP

blimp
chimp
crimp
gimp
imp
limp
primp
scrimp
shrimp
skimp

IN

been
bin
chin
fin
gin
grin
in
inn
kin
Lynn
pin
shin
sin
skin
spin
thin
tin
twin
win

INCE

chintz
mince
prince
quince
rinse
since
wince

INCH

cinch
clinch
finch
flinch
inch
linch
lynch
pinch
winch

IND

bind
blind
dined (*and past of verbs in INE, such as fined, wined*)
kind
hind
mind
rind
wind

INE

brine
dine
fine
line
mine
nine
pine
shine
shrine
sign
spine
swine
thine
twine
vine
whine
wine

ING

bling
bring
cling
ding
fling
king
ping
ring
sing
sling
spring
sting
string
swing
thing
wing
wring

INGE

binge
cringe
fringe
hinge
singe
tinge
twinge

INK

blink
brink
chink
clink
drink
ink
kink
link
mink
pink
rink
shrink
sink
slink
stink
think
wink
zinc

INT

flint
glint
hint
lint
mint
print
splint
sprint
squint
stint
tint

INX

jinx
lynx
minx
sphinx
thinks (*and add s to other nouns and verbs in INK*)

IP

blip
chip
clip
dip
drip
flip
grip
grippe
gyp
hip
lip
nip
quip
rip
ship
sip
skip
slip
snip
strip
tip
trip
whip
zip

IPE

gripe
hype
pipe
ripe
snipe
stripe
swipe
tripe
type
wipe

IRE

briar
buyer
choir
crier
dire
fire
flyer
friar
fryer
higher
hire
ire
liar
lyre
mire
plier
prior
pyre
sire
spire
squire
tire
wire

IRM

firm
germ
squirm
term
worm

IRTH

berth
birth
dearth
earth
firth
girth

mirth
worth

IS

biz
fizz
friz
his
is
quiz
whiz

ISH

dish
fish
squish
swish
wish

ISK

brisk
disc
disk
frisk
risk
whisk

ISS

bliss
Chris
hiss
kiss
miss
Swiss
this

IST

cyst
fist
gist
grist
list
mist
twist
tryst
whist
wrist

IT

bit
fit
flit
grit
hit
it
kit
knit
lit
mitt
pit
quit
sit
skit
slit
spit
split
wit
zit

ITCH

ditch
hitch
itch
niche
pitch

rich
snitch
switch
twitch
which
witch

ITE

bite
blight
bright
cite
Dwight
fight
flight
fright
height
kite
knight
light
mite
night
plight
quite
right
rite
sight
site
sleight
smite
spite
sprite
tight
trite
white
write

ITZ

bits (*and IT + s,
such as fits, sits*)
blitz
Fritz
grits
it's
spitz
spritz

IVE

Clive
dive
drive
five
hive
I've
live
strive
thrive

IZE

buys
guise
guys
prize
rise
size
wise

OB

blob
Bob
cob
job
fob
knob
lob

94

mob
rob
Rob
snob
sob
swab
throb

OBE

globe
lobe
probe
robe

OCK

block
chock
clock
crock
dock
frock
hock
knock
lock
mock
pock
rock
shock
sock
stock
walk
wok

OD

cod
clod
god
God

nod
odd
plod
pod
prod
rod
quad
scrod
shod
sod
squad
Todd
trod
wad

ODE

bode
bowed
code
goad
hoed
load
mode
ode
road
rode
showed (and
past of verbs in
OW)
toad

OFF

cough
doff
off
scoff
soph
trough

OG

bog
clog
cog
dog
flog
fog
frog
grog
hog
jog
log
nog
Prague
slog

OIL

boil
broil
coil
foil
oil
soil
spoil
toil

OKE

bloke
broke
choke
cloak
coke
croak
folk
joke
oak
poke
smoke
soak

spoke
stoke
stroke
woke
yoke
yolk

OLD

bold
cold
fold
gold
hold
mold
mould
old
scold
sold
told

OLE

bowl
coal
dole
droll
foal
goal
hole
Joel
knoll
mole
pole
poll
role
roll
scroll
sol
sole
soul

stole
stroll
toll
troll
whole

OLT

bolt
colt
dolt
jolt
volt

OM

bomb
from
prom
Tom

OME

chrome
comb
dome
foam
gnome
home
loam
Nome
ohm
roam
Rome
tome

ON

con
don
Don
gone

95

John
Jon
on
Ron
swan

OND
blonde
bond
pond
wand

ONE
bone
blown
cone
drone
flown
groan
grown
hone
Joan
known
loan
lone
moan
own
phone
prone
sewn
shown
sown
stone
throne
tone
zone

ONG
gong
long
prong
song
strong
thong
throng
tong
wrong

OOD
could
good
hood
should
stood
wood
would

OOF
goof
hoof
proof
roof
spoof
woof

OOK
book
brook
cook
crook
hook
look
nook
rook
shook
took

OOL
cool
drool
fool
ghoul
jewel
pool
rule
school
spool
stool
tool
who'll

OOM
bloom
boom
broom
doom
flume
fume
gloom
groom
loom
plume
room
tomb
whom

OON
boon
croon
dune
June
loon
moon
noon
prune
soon

spoon
strewn
swoon
tune

OOP
coop
croup
droop
dupe
goop
group
hoop
loop
scoop
soup
stoop
swoop
troop
troupe
whoop

OOR
boor
moor
poor
sewer
sure
tour

OOSE
Bruce
deuce
goose
juice
loose
moose
mousse
noose

spruce
truce
use
Zeus

OOT
boot
brute
chute
flute
fruit
hoot
jute
loot
moot
root
route
shoot
soot
suit
toot

OOTH
booth
Ruth
sleuth
tooth
truth
youth

OOVE
groove
move
prove
you've

OOZE
blues

brews (and add
s to other nouns
and verbs in
EW, such as
chews, dues)
bruise
choose
cruise
lose
ooze
ruse
shoes
snooze
who's
whose

OP

bop
chop
cop
crop
drop
flop
glop
hop
mop
plop
pop
prop
shop
swap
top

OPE

cope
grope
hope
lope
mope

pope
rope
scope
slope
soap

OR

boar
bore
core
corps
door
floor
for
fore
four
gore
lore
more
nor
or
ore
pore
pour
roar
soar
score
snore
store
swore
Thor
tore
wore
yore
your
you're

ORD

bored (and past
of verbs in OR)
gourd
hoard
horde
sword

ORM

dorm
form
norm
storm
swarm
warm

ORN

born
borne
corn
horn
morn
mourn
scorn
shorn
sworn
thorn
torn
warn
worn

ORSE

coarse
course
force
hoarse
horse
Morse

Norse
source

ORT

court
fort
forte
port
quart
short
snort
sort
sport
thwart
tort
wart

OSE

beaus
bows
chose
close
clothes
doze
froze
hoes
hose
nose
pose
prose
rose
Rose
those
woes

OSS

boss
cross

floss
gloss
loss
moss
Ross
sauce
toss

OST (SHORT)

cost
crossed (and
past of verbs in
OSS, such as
tossed)
frost
lost

OST (LONG)

boast
coast
ghost
host
most
post
roast
toast

OT

blot
clot
cot
dot
Dot
got
hot
jot
knot
lot
not

plot
pot
rot
Scot
Scott
shot
slot
spot
squat
swat
tot
trot
watt
what
yacht

OTCH
blotch
botch
notch
Scotch
splotch
swatch
watch

OTE
bloat
boat
coat
dote
float
goat
gloat
groat
moat
note
oat
quote

rote
smote
throat
tote
vote
wrote

OUCH
couch
crouch
grouch
ouch
pouch
slouch
vouch

OUD
cloud
crowd
loud
proud
shroud

OUGHT
bought
brought
caught
ought
sought
taught
taut
thought

OUNCE
bounce
flounce
ounce

pounce
trounce

OUND
bound
crowned
found
ground
hound
mound
pound
round
sound
wound

OUR
cower
dour
flour
flower
hour
our
power
scour
shower
sour
tower

OUSE
blouse
douse
grouse
house
louse
mouse
souse
spouse

OUT
bout
clout
doubt
drought
flout
gout
grout
out
pout
rout
scout
shout
snout
spout
sprout
stout
tout
trout

OVE (UV)
dove
glove
love
of
shove

OVE (OHV)
cove
dove
drove
grove
rove
stove
strove
trove
wove

OVE (OOV)
groove
move
prove
who've
you've

OW
bough
bow
brow
chow
cow
frau
how
now
plough
plow
prow
row
scow
sow
thou
vow
wow

OW (OH)
beau
blow
bow
crow
do (music tone)
doe
dough
Flo
floe
flow
foe

fro
glow
go
grow
ho
hoe
Joe
Jo
know
lo
low
mow
no
O
oh
owe
pro
roe
row
sew
show
slow
snow
so
sow
stow
though
throw
toe
tow
whoa
woe

OWL

cowl
foul
fowl
growl
howl

jowl
owl
prowl
scowl
yowl

OWN

brown
clown
crown
down
drown
frown
gown
noun
town

OWZE

browse
drowse
rouse

OX

box
clocks *(and add s to any OCK word)*
fox
ox
sox

OY

boy
buoy
cloy
coy
joy
ploy

soy
toy

UB

club
cub
drub
dub
grub
hub
nub
rub
scrub
snub
sub
tub

UCH

clutch
crutch
hutch
much
such
touch

UCK

buck
chuck
Chuck
cluck
duck
luck
pluck
puck
Puck
struck
stuck
suck

truck
tuck

UD

blood
bud
Bud
cud
dud
flood
mud
spud
stud
thud

UDE

brood
brewed
crude
cued
dude
feud
food
Jude
mood
prude
rude
shrewd
you'd
who'd

UDGE

budge
drudge
fudge
grudge
judge
nudge

sludge
smudge
trudge

UFF

bluff
buff
cuff
duff
fluff
gruff
guff
huff
muff
puff
rough
ruff
scruff
scuff
snuff
stuff
tough

UG

bug
chug
drug
dug
hug
jug
lug
mug
plug
pug
rug
shrug
slug
smug
snug

thug
tug

UL
cull
dull
gull
hull
lull
mull
null
scull
skull

ULE
fuel
mule
you'll
yule

ULK
bulk
hulk
skulk
sulk

ULL
bull
full
pull
wool

UM
chum
come
crumb
drum

dumb
from
glum
gum
hum
mum
numb
plum
plumb
rum
scum
slum
some
strum
sum
swum
thrum
thumb

UMP
bump
chump
clump
dump
frump
grump
hump
jump
lump
plump
pump
rump
slump
stump
thump
ump

UN
bun
done
dun
fun
gun
none
nun
one
pun
run
shun
son
spun
stun
sun
ton
won

UNCH
brunch
bunch
crunch
hunch
lunch
munch
punch
scrunch

UNG
clung
flung
hung
lung
rung
slung
sprung
strung

stung
sung
swung
tongue
wrung
young

UNK
bunk
chunk
drunk
flunk
hunk
junk
monk
plunk
shrunk
skunk
sunk
trunk

UNT
blunt
brunt
bunt
front
grunt
hunt
punt
runt
shunt
stunt

UP
cup
pup
sup
up

URCH
birch
church
lurch
perch
search
smirch

URD
bird
curd
gird
heard
herd
third
word

URE
cure
fewer
lure
newer
pure
sewer
skewer
sure
your
you're

URK
clerk
Dirk
irk
jerk
lurk
perk
quirk
shirk

smirk
Turk
work

URL

curl
earl
Earl
girl
furl
hurl
pearl
purl
swirl
whirl

URN

Berne
burn
churn
earn
fern
learn
spurn
stern
tern

turn
urn
yearn

URST

burst
first
thirst
worst

US

bus
fuss
Gus
muss
plus
pus
Russ
thus
us

USE

fuse
muse
news
use

USH

blush
brush
crush
flush
gush
hush
mush
plush
rush
shush
thrush

UST

crust
dust
just
lust
must
rust
trust

UTE

beaut
butte
Butte

cute
lute
mute
suit

Y

aye
buy
by
bye
cry
die
dry
dye
eye
fly
fry
guy
Guy
hi
high
I
lie
lye
my
pie
pry

rye
shy
sigh
sky
sly
spry
spy
sty
Thai
thigh
thy
tie
vie
why
wry
Y

RHYME-A-TON WORD GAMES

1. Pick any word out of a rhyme group and use it in a sentence.

    ET: "My *pet* is a dog."

2. Pick another word out of the same rhyme group and use it as the action word (verb) in a sentence.

    "I *met* my next-door neighbor yesterday."

3. Pick two rhymes out of another rhyme group and create a sentence.

    OTE: "I *wrote* a short *note* to my sister."

4. Make up sentences using at least three rhyming words from any group.

    AD: "*Brad* saw his *dad* and both of them were *glad*."

    ILL: "*Bill* was *ill* so he took a *pill* from the doctor."

    UM: "My *chum* was *glum* until I gave her a *plum*."

5. Make up two connecting sentences (almost a mini-story) using any combination of four or more words from a rhyme group.

    AKE: "The car began to *shake*, so *Blake* put on the brake. If he hadn't, Blake's car would have gone into the *lake*."

6. Make up two connecting sentences using words from two rhyme groups. The second sentence will use rhymes from the second group. Use four or more rhymes. At least two rhymes from each group must be in each sentence.

    AN + OCK: "*Ann* and *Dan* had a *plan*. They would *walk* to the *dock* right down the *block*."

7. Add another connecting sentence to the first two in activity 6. This sentence must have at least two rhyming words from a third group.

> **OLE: "They took a *stroll* and reached their *goal*."**

8. Add still another connecting sentence to the three sentences you already have from activities 6 and 7. This sentence must include at least two words from a fourth group.

> **UDE: "They were now both in the *mood* to eat some *food*."**

9. Read your four sentences out loud. Continue the connecting sentence rhyme game by adding as many sentences as you wish, making sure that each new sentence includes at least two new words from every new rhyme group.

10. Invent tongue twisters using at least four rhymes from a group.

> **AIN: "*Jane* was in *Maine*. She went in a *plane*. She flew there from *Spain*."**

> **ON: "*John* is *gone*, said *Ron* to *Don*. *John* is *gone*, *Don*, to him said *Ron*."**

11. Find as many examples as you can of two words in a rhyming group that sound exactly the same but are spelled differently. These are called *homophones* (fare and fair; new and knew; heal and heel). If you know the different meanings of the differently spelled words, use each pair in a sentence.

> **"They raised the *fare* on the bus without notice, which wasn't *fair* to the passengers."**

> **"I *knew* that I was getting a *new* book."**

> **"Now that I have a special *heel* on my left shoe, my foot is beginning to *heal*."**

12. Discover as many examples as you can of three homophones in a rhyming group (to, too, two). Use all three words in one or two sentences.

> "The *two* sisters, Laura and Samantha, are going *to* the basketball game. Their brother, Todd, wants *to* go, *too*."

13. Create a mini-story about cooking in the kitchen. Use at least four OIL rhymes.

14. Pick sets of words out of the same rhyming groups and make connections.

> **AG: bag and tag—"Sometimes you have to put a *tag* on a *bag* so it won't get lost."**

> **OOL: cool and pool—"If it's too *cool*, you should not swim in the *pool*."**

15. Pick sets of words, each from different rhyming groups, and make connections.

> **ALK and ITE: "We use *chalk* to *write* on the board."**

> **ALL and EW: "We go to the *mall* to buy something *new*."**

16. Create a two-line poem using any rhyming sound.

> **AY:**

> **The ship docked in the *bay*.**

> **It was a beautiful *day*.**

This two-line poem uses the same rhyme at the end of each line. This rhyming arrangement is called *aa*. If you added two more lines with the same rhyme, it would be an *aaaa* arrangement.

17. Create a poem with four lines. The first and third line will use the same rhyme, and the second and fourth lines will use a different rhyme.

> **AY and EW:**

> **The ship docked in the *bay*.**

The water looked so *blue*.

It was a beautiful *day*.

And overhead birds *flew*.

This four-line poem uses an *abab* rhyming arrangement. If you add two more lines with a third rhyme, you will have an *ababcc* pattern. You can also have *abac abac* or any other arrangement you choose. The possibilities are endless, as endless as the rhymes you may decide to use. Try the ones you've learned so far.

18. Create a mini-story using four rhyme groups that follow each other in the Rhyme-a-ton.

    > **AB, ACE, ACK, ACT: "The men got in the *cab* and told the driver to give *chase*. *Jack* and *Mac* were in the *back*, and their *cab* was right on *track*. They caught up with the other car, and that's not just a story, it's a *fact*."**

19. Pick three or four rhyming groups that follow each other in the Rhyme-a-ton and select a letter from the alphabet, such as *b*. Try to find words that begin with that letter in the selected groups. (AG, AIL, AIN: bag, brag, bail, bale, Braille, bane, brain.) Play this game with as many different letters and rhyming groups that follow each other as you like. Have fun.

20. Make up your own Rhyme-a-ton funny word list, using two words together from the same or different rhyming groups. The words you invent should not make any sense unless you make sense out of them with your own definitions. (UD: budspud, thuddud; ILE: smilemile, stylefile; ARE: harebare, pairsquare; EST + EW: chestblue, restnew, bestdrew.) You may wind up with your own special, secret language. If you pair up with a friend, you can develop this secret language together.

21. Create your own word games from the Rhyme-a-ton. Make up your own rules and your own connections.

You may also be interested in

The Early Literacy Kit: This innovative and practical kit, put together by two well-known specialists in the field of early literacy, contains everything storytime presenters need to spread the word about school readiness skills to adult caregivers of children from birth to age five. Ideal for program planners, this convenient resource will help you teach caregivers how they can promote their children's development in seven important areas.

Storytime Magic: Enriching and supplementing storytelling programs with fingerplays, flannelboards, and other props will be a cinch thanks to this generous sampling of art and craft ideas, songs, and action rhymes. This time-saving resource includes thematic organization to make program planning easy, recommended books for each theme, easy-to-follow craft and flannelboard patterns, and Quick Tips boxes that enhance the early literacy component.

Children's Literature Gems: Master the huge array of excellent children's books from the past and the present with this must-have resource from children's librarian Elizabeth Bird. With her strong passion for children's books and the profession, she will help you build and manage your children's collection, review the basics of storytime, storytelling, and booktalking, identify the 100 children's books that belong in every library, and much more.

Something Musical Happened at the Library: Drawing on thousands of hours of listening and programming, Reid selects the best of the best into eight ready-to-use comprehensive program plans. Use this abundant mix of picture books paired with kid-tested musical recordings to get up to speed fast on making music an everyday part of your programs, to build your own storytimes with innovative and fun pairings of books and recordings, and to enliven any storytime by incorporating simple song types—from call and response to ever-popular rounds.